ABU BAKR

The Pinnacle of Truthfulness

ABU BAKR
The Pinnacle of Truthfulness

Reşit Haylamaz

New Jersey

Copyright © 2013 by Tughra Books
Originally published in Turkish as *Sadâkatin Zirve İsmi Hz. Ebû Bekir* in 2005.

16 15 14 13   3 4 5 6

All rights reserved. No part of this book may be reproduced or transmitted in any form or by any means, electronic or mechanical, including photocopying, recording or by any information storage and retrieval system without permission in writing from the Publisher.

Published by Tughra Books
345 Clifton Ave., Clifton,
NJ, 07011, USA

www.tughrabooks.com

Library of Congress Cataloging-in-Publication Data Available

ISBN: 978-1-59784-250-1

Translated by Omer A. Ergi

Printed by
Çağlayan A.Ş., Izmir - Turkey

TABLE OF CONTENTS

Preface vii
The Environment in Which He Was Raised.................... 1
Name and Title 3
A Popular Profession... 7
Muhammad the Trustworthy 9
Joyful Tidings... 12
They Were All Aware of His Presence........................... 18
Unforgettable Memories 21
Abu Bakr's Social Status in Mecca................................. 23
Heading Towards the Communion............................... 25
The Profit of a Life Time 36
Utilizing His Social Status... 37
Abu Bakr Helps the Poor.. 39
Race to Serve Humanity 43
Journey Towards the Land of Abyssinia...................... 53
The Boycott 59
The Truthful One.. 61
The Holy Migration and the Spirit of Companionship.............. 65
Initial Years in Medina 77
Funhas and Abu Bakr.. 80
Towards the Battle of Badr 83
The Man of the Battle Fields 87
Abu Bakr's Place by the Prophet's Side 90

His Maturity and Ability to Comprehend 95
The Initial Signs of Departure 98
A Man of Trust and Reliability 100
Modesty and Sincerity 103
The Philanthropist 104
The Day of the Conquest 111
The Leader of Pilgrims 115
The Farewell Pilgrimage 116
The Time of Reunion 118
Road to Caliphate 123
Futile Opposition 127
His Attitude Towards Inheritors 129
Hejaz Shaken With Controversy 131
Deterrent Solution to Zakat Violation 133
Incidents of Apostasy 135
False Prophets 136
Usama's Army 138
Peace and Serenity 143
Financial Hardship 145
Piety and Fear of God 148
Reunion with Ummu Ayman 152
Two Years of Profuse Blessings 155
As the Curtains Come Down 156
His Inheritance 161
His Family Life 163

PREFACE

A person is responsible for the duties given to him by the Almighty and His Messenger, no matter what social position he holds in the community. Along with the daily prayers, fasting, giving alms, and performing the holy pilgrimage, deeds such as sharing the beauty of religion with others, warning people about the dead-ends of life, guiding them to a path that leads to eternal happiness, and making an effort to form a social life in which the gentle winds of paradise blow through a holy atmosphere can also be considered as religious obligations. This means that inviting people to the right path is a duty bestowed upon all Muslims, regardless of their gender, rank, or natural disposition.

In relation to this, Abu Bakr, a man who holds the highest point of companionship, can be taken as an example. From the moment he met the noble Messenger, Abu Bakr became a role model for humanity. His captivating life story begins at the local marketplace. It is a life of epic struggle that would eventually raise him to the rank of Caliphate. Abu Bakr's inspiring story of perseverance, endurance, and triumph serves as the best paradigm for Muslims of today.

Giving your entire wealth away when it was needed is an inimitable virtue. In addition to this, giving up your precious life in the name of the One who bestows life is a virtue that honors you with immortality. Those who attain such a unique level of virtue will be exempted from the corrosion exerted by time and space. Furthermore, they will set sail towards a majestic realm granted by the true Owner of space and time. How could such an honor be achieved? Here is a life that serves as an example. May we all benefit from the life story of Abu Bakr, the symbol of Loyalty!

THE ENVIRONMENT IN WHICH HE WAS RAISED

His father was Uthman Ibn Amr (Abu Kuhafa), and his was mother Salma Bint Sahr (Ummu'l Khayr). He was born three years after the famous Elephant Incident, when Abraha, the king of Yemen, planned to overrun Mecca with his army of elephants. Abu Bakr's mother was also the daughter of Abu Kuhafa's uncle. During this period, Salma, called "the mother of blessings" by the people of Mecca, was going through a difficult time because all of the male children she had given birth to had died.

The desire to have a boy child was burning in her compassionate heart. Two years had passed since the Elephant incident, and Salma was pregnant again. The excitement could clearly be seen in her eyes. This time, she had great anticipation in her heart. She was almost certain that this baby would be a boy. However, she felt compelled to do something extra so that her wish for a baby boy would come true. Consequently, she made a pledge that her son would serve the Ka'ba if he lived. She announced her decision publicly. In those days, this type of oath was considered as a promise that had to be fulfilled.

Finally, the mother of blessings began to feel the pains of labor. The time had arrived, and she was about to give birth to a blessed child. Although she was almost certain that this time she would give birth to a baby boy, she continued to have reservations. The reason for anxiety was giving birth to a son did not mean that he would live. She vowed that soon after her son was born, she would face the Ka'ba and make a sincere prayer to her Lord. Her intention was to make the following prayer: "Oh Lord! Grant my beloved child a life from death. Save him for my sake!"[1]

The level of sincerity in one's prayer was the most obvious sign for acceptance. Certainly, such a deep entreaty could not be turned down; Abu Kuhafa's son was born alive.

---

[1] Ibn Hajar, *el-Isaba*, 4/171

NAME AND TITLE

The mother of blessings was not a woman who would dishonor her oath. It was time to select a name for the newborn. She named her son Abdul Ka'ba, which meant the servant of the Ka'ba. Abu Kuhafa did not object to this because the Ka'ba was a place that people revered. Moreover, the ghastly fate of Abraha's army that came to destroy it was not forgotten.

How could one disrespect the Ka'ba? It was the first ever shrine on earth, built in the name of God. At the same time, the Ka'ba was a place that reminded you of God. Whenever, the name of God was mentioned, people thought of the Ka'ba. For this reason, Abu Kuhafa would often call his son by the name of Abdullah, which meant the servant of God. He wished that his son would become a true servant of the Ka'ba.

They lived in a society where women had no value thus only the views and perspectives of men were taken seriously. For this reason, the name selected by Salma was already forgotten and Mecca came to know the new arrival as Abdullah Ibn Uthman. It was a name chosen by Abu Kuhafa.

This was also a culture that recognized people by their titles. Therefore, he was given the title of "Ateeq" because, unlike the other babies before him, he had survived. Moreover, he came from a noble bloodline. The word Ateeq meant "a person who walked to freedom from captivity." It was also translated as "a person who deviated from the path of those who came before him and survived."

Those days, everyone agreed that the title suited Abdullah Ibn Uthman simply because Ateeq also carried the meaning of beauty, and those who gazed upon Abdullah's glowing face were filled with admiration. The Arabic language is rich in context, so the word Ateeq was not limited to these interpretations. It was also used for people who held the first spot in the race for generosity. Without doubt, Abu Bakr would always be the undisputed winner in this race.

Eventually, he would be acknowledged as Abu Bakr, which meant "the father of Bakr." It is not known where this title actually came from since Abu Bakr never had a son named Bakr. However, when we analyze the meaning of Bakr, we may be able to make some predictions. Meanings such as to rush, to lead, the first drop of rain, early morning, reaching the earliest time of prayer, reaching the beginning of the sermon, honey made from the initial flowers of spring, the first fruit of the tree, and a productive soil may all be derived from the root of the word Bakr.

According to another view this word is also used to describe a large, powerful clan. When we analyze the word from a terminological perspective, we conclude that almost all of the translations above carry a common meaning of being first. Consequently, no matter where the title comes from or what sort of meaning it carries, Abu Bakr's title concurs with his unique life story. He was the first man to embrace the faith and provide support to the noble Messenger of God, peace and blessings be upon him. Moreover, he was also the leading individual in many of the movements and activities initiated by the noble Prophet. Everyone agrees that the name Abu Bakr holds the first spot by the side of the Prophet.

The sultan of Loyalty, who was known by the names, Abdul Ka'ba, Abdullah, Ateeq, and Abu Bakr would forget his title Abdul Ka'ba, following the day he testified to the Oneness of God in the presence of the noble Messenger. His embrace of Islam had taken place soon after the Prophet's reunion at Mt Hira. Following his inclusion to Islam, the noble Prophet would address him as Abdullah and referred to him as Ateeq, a man who has saved himself from hellfire.

One day, the noble Messenger had seen Abu Bakr approaching from a distance. He turned to those around him and said: "If any of you wish to see a man who has saved himself from hellfire, take a look at the person who approaches."[2]

The most appropriate attribute that matched with the name Abu Bakr was the title of Siddiq, meaning "the truthful one." Sometime later, Abu Bakr would be recognized by this title only. He had taken the first step on this path, and he had made the most ground in relation to loy-

---

[2] Hakim, *Mustadrak*, 3/64 (4404)

alty and fidelity. Just as he did with his life, he had also become an example, with his name and title, for those who followed.

In addition to this, he was given the titles of "Sahib,"[3] for his friendship in the cave described by the holy Qur'an; "Atqa,"[4] for the attribute that the Qur'an uses for those who spend their wealth on the holy path and to emancipate the slaves; "The second one of the two,"[5] the sentence used by the holy Qur'an to describe their stay in the cave during Hijrah; and "Awwah,"[6] for his sensitive nature, compassion, fear, and depth in submitting to God.

---

[3] Tawba 9:40
[4] Layl, 92:17
[5] Tawba, 9:40
[6] Ibn Sa'd, *Tabaqatu'l-Kubra*, 3/170

A POPULAR PROFESSION

Mecca was a city renowned for its merchants and trade. In particular, the Quraysh conducted business throughout the year by sending trade-caravans to Yemen and Damascus. Since these were the conditions in Mecca, most teenagers would hang out at the marketplace to gain experience in trade and business.

Abu Bakr was also a young man who had left his childhood behind to join the trade-caravans that frequently traveled to Yemen and Damascus. Being a successful merchant required certain skills, and Abu Bakr possessed them more than any other. Abu Bakr formed a sense of trust and closeness in the hearts of those he visited and a feeling of reliability for those who visited him. He did not approach the trade business as a one of venture. Neither did he use his wealth to oppress others. For this reason, he had become the sought after man in the trade business. In no time, Abu Bakr's capital had increased to forty thousand dirhams.[7]

Abu Bakr was not only recognized for his skills in business dealings, but he was also acknowledged for his unique manners and good behavior. He displayed a different kind

---

[7] Ibn Ebi Shayba, *Musannaf*, 7/12 (33862)

of maturity compared to those in the same age group. In contrast to the other young men, he would not stand before the idols to beg for help, he did not drink wine, and he abstained from all forms of adultery.

Even in an environment of ignorance, no one could find a fault in Abu Bakr or criticize him for an inappropriate behavior. He had remained so pure that the only thing the non-believers disapproved of was his faith.

MUHAMMAD THE TRUSTWORTHY

There was a person in Mecca whom Abu Bakr imitated with longing. This individual's virtues became more obvious with each passing day, and people had begun to address him as "the Trustworthy" (al-Amin). Although, some continued to address him as Muhammad, the majority of Meccans joined the name with his title and called him "Muhammad the Trustworthy."

Muhammad the Trustworthy was two years older than Abu Bakr. For this reason, Abu Bakr respected him also as an older brother. Muhammad and Abu Bakr had grown up together simply because Mecca was a small town, and everyone knew each other in those days. The people of Mecca were used to seeing the two together, so everyone was aware of the solid friendship that existed between the two. His mother, Ummu Salamah once stated, "They were like twin brothers."[8]

They were also similar in character and disposition. For this reason, they had established a solid friendship from the first day they had met. Abu Bakr enjoyed life when he was with Muhammad but when he left Mecca for business purposes, he would long for his beloved friend through-

---

[8] Khaled Muhammad, *Jae Abu Bakr*, 30

out the trip. Muhammad was the first person he visited upon his return. Muhammad the Trustworthy was a person unlike any other. He gave a sense of indescribable reliance to those who befriended him. Muhammad's presence gave great pleasure to Abu Bakr. For this reason, he felt an additional joy when he found out that Muhammad was joining the next trade caravan out of Mecca. This was a great opportunity for Abu Bakr. During the trip, he experienced moments that he would never forget for the rest of his life. Abu Bakr was in the caravan led by Muhammad the Trustworthy. The caravan that headed towards Damascus belonged to Khadija the Pure. An incident they witnessed even before they left Mecca was a sign of the many incredible events they would encounter during the journey. As they commenced their journey under the roasting heat of the desert sun, a small cloud appeared above Muhammad's head. The mysterious cloud followed Muhammad providing a shade that protected him from the intense heat of the desert sun. During the course of the journey, Abu Bakr also had the privilege of listening to the joyful tidings of the Christian Monk, Nastura. The Monk implied that Muhammad the Trustworthy was the last Prophet for whom the people have been waiting for a long time. Along with Maysara, Abu Bakr also listened with tears as the Christian Monk talked about the man who was sitting under the shade of a tree.

The news about Muhammad was no surprise because his manners in business trades and in general gave everyone a sense of reliance. As he fulfilled every promise he made with extreme sensitivity, his unique manners were reflected by the entire caravan. Just like Muhammad, the trade caravan also became an entity that everyone trusted.

The stories Abu Bakr heard from the wise old man, Waraqa remained fresh in his mind. In an era when the darkness of ignorance had covered their society like a thick blanket, there were a few people who talked about the emergence of the light. The stories he heard from these people, plus the extraordinary incidents he witnessed during their journey, pointed to the same individual. This individual was none other than his beloved friend Muhammad.

Following Muhammad's marriage to Khadija, the bonds of their friendship grew stronger because they were also neighbors now. The new developments enabled Abu Bakr to interact with Muhammad more often. They lived on the same street because Muhammad had moved into the house of Khadija.

In addition to this, they were also related according to their family trees. The name, Murrah Ibn Ka'b was recorded in the family trees of both Muhammad and Abu Bakr.

JOYFUL TIDINGS

Indeed, he lived in a century in which ignorance was at its peak. The negative incidents occurring all around oppressed the observers' spiritual world. However, this did not mean there was no progress in the name of virtue and righteousness. Although, small in numbers, there were still people who had declared war against ignorance and idolatry. These people constantly spoke about righteousness and morals. Abu Bakr had great interest in these people and frequently joined their gatherings. In particular, he enjoyed visiting individuals such as Waraqa, Zaid Ibn Amr, and Kuss Ibn Saida. The eyes of these people were always focused on the heavens above. They were looking for the last Messenger of God, who would invite humanity to salvation. This was the common issue that strengthened and increased their love for one another. They were using the language of poetry to talk about Him and announce His name to those around them.

One day, Abu Bakr heard a conversation which took place between Zaid Ibn Amr[9] and Umayya Ibn Abi's-

---

[9] Zaid Ibn Amr was one of the people who gave the joyful tidings of the last Prophet. When the Prophet's arrival was delayed, he believed that he may have come to another region. He left Mecca

Salt.[10] Zaid said to Umayya: "No religion has legitimacy and value on the Day of Judgment, apart from God's verdict and being a Hanif (those days, people who believed in one God, the God of Abraham, were called Hanif)." Zaid continued in a serious tone, "Be cautious! Will the awaited Prophet emerge from our society or from the land of Palestine?"[11]

Abu Bakr listened vigilantly to the conversation which took place between the two friends. They were talking about issues from another world, and this conversation could not be taken lightly. Moreover, these two were amongst the most astute in Mecca.

The conversation had formed a great curiosity in Abu Bakr's mind. Quickly, he went to Waraqa Ibn Nawfal, who was another person of wisdom. He was a man whose eyes were fixed on the heavens above. Abu Bakr sat next to him and explained everything he heard at the Ka'ba. Then he asked Waraqa what it all meant. Waraqa said: "Oh the son of my brother!" His sincerity was easily detected in his tone of voice as he continued, "The people of the Book and scholars concur on the fact that the last Prophet will emerge from the heart of the Arab society. I have good knowledge in genealogy. Your clan comes from the heart of the Arab family tree."

With his words, Waraqa drew Abu Bakr's attention to his own clan. In fact, he was advising him to look for the

---

in search of the Prophet and was killed on the journey. Ibn Sa'd, *Tabaqatu'l-Kubra*, 3/379, Ibn Hajar, *Tahzebu't-Tahzeb*, 3/364

[10] Umayya was a poet from the era of ignorance. Ibn Hajar, *el-Isaba*, 1/249

[11] Suyuti, *el-Hasaisu'l-Kubra*, 1/42

awaited one in his own clan. Upon hearing this, Abu Bakr asked: "Oh uncle! What will this Prophet bring and what will he claim?"

Waraqa replied: "He will say the things that will be said to him. When he arrives, tyranny and the medium for oppression will vanish."[12]

On another occasion, Abu Bakr heard Zaid ibn Amr say:

> Oh the people of the Quraysh! I swear by the One who holds my soul in His hand, no one amongst you follows Abraham, apart from me! Now, I wait for the arrival of a Prophet from the family tree of Ishmael. I hope that I live to see him.

Another old man known by the title of Amr Ibn Rabia had heard Zaid and replied, "If you live to see him, give him my regards also!"[13]

If these wise old men were telling the truth, then the people of Mecca faced many imminent surprises. They were so certain in their predictions that the news was impossible to ignore. Moreover, they all suggested the arrival of the last Prophet.

From that point on, Abu Bakr's perspective on many issues had changed. From time to time, he would visit the Ka'ba to observe the deplorable conditions in which some people lived. Abu Bakr believed that worshiping the idols

---

[12] Hindi, *Kenzu'l-Ummal*, 1/2483 (35357)
[13] Ibn Hajar, *Tahzebu't-Tahzeb*, 3/364

was a superstition, and he had no hesitation in reminding himself of this fact.

The stories he heard from the wise men had been depriving him of sleep. Even his dreams were ornamented with the notion of following the awaited Prophet. How could he have thought any other way? All the wise men he visited played the same tune and all of his friends sang the same lyrics.

On one side, there were people writing prescriptions to save humanity from moral bankruptcy. On the other, there were those describing the awaited Prophet in detail. They were so specific in their descriptions that even his title amongst the people and the characteristics of those who would support him were mentioned.

One day Abu Bakr went to Damascus for trade purposes. During his stay at Damascus, he had an intriguing dream. In his dream, the moon was broken into pieces. Then it had descended to enter every house in Mecca. The pieces then joined back together to form a full moon which finally settled in Abu Bakr's house. He woke up screaming. The dream had given him so much elation that he could not hold himself back anymore.

Abu Bakr decided to find out what the dream meant, so he visited a righteous monk. He explained everything he had seen. The monk became extremely thrilled as he listened to Abu Bakr's dream. Then he said: "Without doubt, his day has come!" Abu Bakr was confused. He wanted a dream interpretation from this man, yet he was talking about something that Abu Bakr did not comprehend. Once again, he asked: "What are you talking about?" Although Abu Bakr's eyes indicated that he had some idea about the monk's implication, he wanted a confirmation. Abu Bakr continued with another question: "Are you talking about the awaited Prophet?" Initially, the monk nodded his head, and then he replied: "Yes! You will embrace his faith, and you will be his greatest supporter amongst all human beings."[14]

During his journey back from Damascus, Abu Bakr had one thing on his mind, the last Prophet. From time to time, he would raise his hands in the air and shout: "Who will recite a poem from Umayya Ibn Abi-Salt?" A person from the caravan replied: "Umayya has so many poems, which one would you like us to recite?" Abu Bakr replied: "Verily! We have our own Prophet." Upon Abu Bakr's request, one person from the caravan began to recite the poem:

> Verily! We have our own Prophet. He shall bring us news from tomorrow!
> We are certain, if there was no benefit in wisdom, we would have been butchered by swords.
> Oh Lord! Protect me from polytheism and fill my heart with faith for as long as the world stands.
> For I seek refuge from all evil, in the One and only creator, for whom the people carry the banner of religion and perform their pilgrimage.[15]

---

[14] Abu Ja'far et-Tabari, *er-Riyadu'n-Nadera*, 1/413 (333)
[15] Ali Muhammad, *el-Inshirahu wa rafu'd-diki bi sireti Abi Bakr as-Siddiq*, p. 34

Their path on the way back to Mecca passed from the region of Busra, where a priest named Bahira lived. Abu Bakr wished to explain his dream to Bahira. So he quickly went to the monastery in which the priest resided.

Abu Bakr explained the dream he had in Damascus. Bahira's eyes were wide open as he listened and he asked where Abu Bakr was from. "Mecca," Abu Bakr calmly replied. It was quite obvious that Bahira needed more information. Hence he asked: "What part of Mecca and which clan?" "The Quraysh," said Abu Bakr with a confused expression on his face. This answer was not enough to satisfy the priest, so he continued his questioning: "What do you do for living?" "I am in the trade business, replied Abu Bakr."

At this point of the conversation, Bahira began to say things that would finally satisfy Abu Bakr's curiosity. "Without doubt, God will make your dream come true! Soon a Prophet will emerge from your clan. You will be his Vizier throughout his life, and after his death, you will be his Caliph!"

Abu Bakr was mesmerized by what he had heard. He did not know what to ask anymore. He felt humbled upon hearing such a clear statement that gave him such an honor. Since his name was mentioned in Bahira's predictions, he decided that he would not tell anyone about this. He would keep it a secret until the day of reunion.[16]

---

[16] Abu Ja'far at-Tabari, *er-Riyadu'n-Nadera*, 1/413 (333)

THEY WERE ALL AWARE OF HIS PRESENCE

With each passing day, Abu Bakr realized that he was getting closer to the Prophet. This feeling gave him a great sense of familiarity. The awaited Prophet's presence was so conspicuous that he was like a full moon rising upon total darkness. Meccans were also aware of this.

Following a lengthy debate, the Meccans had decided to restore the Ka'ba which had been subjected to years of erosion. In those days, the Ka'ba was a great source of income. Each year, people visited the Ka'ba in great numbers. This provided a significant increase in business dealings and brought noteworthy profits. Although perspectives and practices regarding the essence of the Ka'ba had been altered quite significantly, it was still considered as a sacred place.

The restoration was complete, and it was time to place the holy stone of Hajar ul-Aswad back to its original position. Suddenly, an unexpected conflict erupted amongst the different Arab clans. Each clan believed that the honor of placing the stone belonged to them. As the arguments began to escalate, they heard the powerful voice of Umayya.

He proposed a solution. He suggested the first person that entered the Ka'ba should be assigned as a referee.

Umayya was one of their chieftains. He was also a wise old man whose opinion was respected. They left everything aside and keenly waited for someone to enter the Ka'ba. Abu Bakr was also amongst the crowd. Before long, they heard footsteps. It was obvious that someone was approaching. They all had their eyes fixed on the entrance. There was a sense of anxiety in the air. Who was this person that would make the final decision on placing the sacred stone of Hajar ul-Aswad?

Suddenly, one of the men began to shout with excitement: "The Trustworthy! Muhammad the Trustworthy!"

They had already agreed on obeying the ruling of the first person that entered the Ka'ba. However, this person being Muhammad removed all concern and anxiety from their minds. Muhammad had no idea about the latest developments. Therefore, they explained to him every detail of the dispute. Then they asked him to find a solution. Muhammad the Trustworthy said: "Bring me a piece of cloth!"

They rushed and found a piece of cloth. Although, they did not know why he had requested this, they had total confidence in him. If Muhammad the Trustworthy was asking for something, he had a logical reason. The cloth was spread on the ground, and the sacred stone was placed on it. Then Muhammad said, "Each chieftain shall hold from one side of the cloth and lift the stone![17]

---

[17] Ahmed b. Hanbal, *el-Musnad*, 3/425

It was a wonderful solution, for each clan would be honored with lifting the stone. The stone was finally raised by the leaders of the various clans. It had reached the position where it would be placed. Then, Muhammad grabbed the stone with his noble hands and pushed it into its original spot. The ruling had prevented a conflict that may have turned into violence. At the same time, this sacred stone that had been carried by many prophets in the past was, once again, placed in its spot by the hands of a prophet. This was the will of God.

Abu Bakr watched the entire incident with amazement as his mind took him years back to the marketplace at Ukaz. He remembered the words uttered by the old man, Kuss Ibn Saida: "Without doubt, time will come when destiny is fulfilled and the book is revealed!"[18]

Indeed, the will of God had prevailed, and destiny would be fulfilled. Without question, Abu Bakr was the happiest person in regards to the solution of the problem.

---

[18] Halebi, *es-Siratu'l-Halebiyya*, 1/319

UNFORGETTABLE MEMORIES

Many years later, the Messenger of God turned to his followers and asked if anyone amongst them had met Kuss Ibn Saida and had taken advice from him. The silence of the crowd was broken by his dearest friend, Abu Bakr: "Oh noble Messenger of God, I remember it like yesterday."

Then he continued to explain: "I was at the marketplace of Ukaz. Ibn Saida sat on his well-fed gray camel as he spoke to the crowd":

> Oh people! Listen to me well, memorize my words and benefit from what you learn!
>
> All living beings will perish; they will leave this world, never to return again.
>
> Without doubt, there are many signs upon the heavens and proofs on earth from which we need to derive a lesson.
>
> The surface of the earth is like a prepared bed and the heavens above resemble a roof.
>
> The stars are constantly swimming away.
>
> And the seas do not vanish through vaporization.
>
> Gaze upon the nights that wear a black garment.
>
> And the constellation of the zodiac upon the heavens!

> I vow that there is a religion by the side of God, and it is more beautiful than the one you are in now! God has a messenger, whose arrival is near. His shadow is upon us, and the time of his arrival has come.
>
> I ask you why the people who leave this world never return again.
>
> Could it be that they are contented with the place they are in now or were they forsaken into an eternal sleep?
>
> Without doubt, time will come when destiny is fulfilled, and the book is revealed![19]

How could Abu Bakr forget such an incident? As he realized that the noble Messenger was pleased with his story, he recited a poem from Kuss Ibn Saida.

It was obvious that Abu Bakr had no reservations about the arrival of the Last Prophet. He believed this with all his heart. Perhaps, if he had known how close he was to him from the beginning, humanity would have witnessed an example of an extraordinary loyalty and fidelity from the first moment Abu Bakr met him.

---

[19] Halebi, *es-Siratu'l-Halebiyya*, 1/319

ABU BAKR'S SOCIAL STATUS IN MECCA

Due to his success in the trade business, Abu Bakr became a wealthy businessman. Apart from his wealth, he had also earned the respect of the community through his honesty and integrity. His economic power was immense, and his reputation amongst the Quraysh had reached its peak.

He was amongst the leading group of men in Mecca. He was a respected chieftain of Mecca and a member of a group of elite men who made decisions and rulings in Mecca. Abu Bakr was also amongst the committee that consisted of Abu Sufyan, Umayya Ibn Halaf, Utba and Shayba brothers, Abu Jahl, Suhayl Ibn Amr, and Abu Lahab. No decision would be finalized without the vote of Abu Bakr.

With his good manners and wisdom, Abu Bakr became a man of commendation. Amongst the Quraysh, he was the most knowledgeable person in genealogy. Even serious matters such as blood-money and punishment according to retaliation would be brought before him to be dealt with. He had made a reputation with his honesty. He acted with great sensitivity in protecting the rights of others and never treated anyone unfairly. For this reason only, the Quraysh preferred his advice over the views of the other chieftains.

At the same time, Abu Bakr was one the few individuals who had refrained from the negatives of the era of ignorance. This was a quality that separated him from the others. Even though the ugly face of ignorance had taken control of this society, it could not penetrate Abu Bakr's virtuous soul. His relationship with the idols had never been good. Even as a child when his father took him to the Ka'ba, he would watch in perplexity how people worshipped objects that they had made with their own hands. Chastity and purity were important essentials for him. He had made a promise to himself that he would never consume alcohol. He knew that alcohol consumption would beget evil hence he would frequently argue that those who consumed alcohol would eventually lose their honor and munificence.[20]

---

[20] Abu Ja'far et-Tabari, *er-Riyadu'n-Nadera*, 2/146

HEADING TOWARDS THE COMMUNION

Finally, destiny had taken him to Yemen. There he visited a wise old man who had profound knowledge about the Torah and the Bible. Just as the others, he was also waiting for the eternal sun to rise. Upon seeing Abu Bakr, the old man became excited and began to act in peculiar manner. His face had gone pale as he froze like an iceberg. Staring directly into Abu Bakr's eyes, he could not wait any longer to satisfy his curiosity: "I believe you are from the people of Haram!"

They had not spoken a word, yet the old man knew that Abu Bakr was from Mecca. What kind of wisdom was this? The old man wanted to confirm his prediction. Abdullah replied: "Yes, I am from the people of Haram!" The old man was in shock. It seemed as if he had attained something that he had been longing for many years. He wanted to keep the conversation going as he continued to ask: "I guess that you are also from the Quraysh!" Once again, Abu Bakr replied calmly: "Yes, I am from the Quraysh."

The old man's questions did not end there. It was obvious that he had not obtained the information he needed to know. Therefore, he asked another question: "God knows, maybe you come from the Taim clan of the Quraysh?" It was quite obvious that the line of questioning would continue. Abu Bakr realized that the old man wished to know everything about him. The old man felt like a prying individual asking series of private questions to a man he had just met. His face reflected a sense of reservation, yet he had to make another move. So he said: "There is only one more thing that I need to know about you."

Abu Bakr was confused. Why was the old man asking so many questions about his background? He had never met this old man before. However, Abu Bakr did not wish to transgress the limits of respect, so he replied: "What do you wish to know?"

Abu Bakr's composure calmed the old man down. The old man from Yemen realized that his requests would be complied. He gathered his confidence and asked if Abu Bakr could show his stomach to him. Abu Bakr thought this was a bit too much. He was a man of decency, so without any hesitation, he replied: "This I cannot do!" How could he do this? At first, this old man whom he had never met before asked him a number of personal questions. Now, he was asking him to lift his shirt so that he could look at his stomach.

The old man felt extremely embarrassed and disappointed upon seeing the expression on Abu Bakr's face. Abu Bakr was a sensitive person who did not wish to break the old man's heart. For a brief moment, he thought to himself. Perhaps the old man had a good reason. Maybe he knew something, and this is why he was so insistent. Breaking the heart of an elderly person was not appropriate behavior for Abu Bakr. "Okay," he said. Then he added: "But, you must tell me why you ask this of me."

The old man felt comforted now. This was an important opportunity for him. Everything began to run smoothly as the old man began to explain his reasons:

> Genuine knowledge and reliable sources taught me that the last Prophet of God would emerge from the region of Haram. Initially, he will be supported by a young man and a mature individual. The young man who stands by his side will possess virtues such as benevolence, courage, aptitude, and good manners. In order to protect the Prophet, he will solve difficult problems, and he will be willing to sacrifice himself.[21]
>
> The other person who will support him is a slender individual with white complexion. He is a kind man who has a soft heart. He has a mole on his stomach and a mark above his knee. If you comply with my request, then I will be certain of your attributes. However, if you refuse, my prediction will not be confirmed.

By now, Abu Bakr's curiosity was no different to that of the old man's. He did not know what to say. Indeed, he had heard many times before about the awaited Prophet, but never in such detail. The old man was not only talking

---

[21] The attributes described here indicate Ali ibn Abi Talib, the hero of benevolence who stood by the side of the Prophet from the first day they met.

about the coming of the last Prophet, but he was describing the characteristics of the initial team that would be formed around the Prophet. Moreover, he was suggesting that Abu Bakr would be amongst them. Abu Bakr's curiosity had significantly increased. In order to satisfy his curiosity, he had to expose his stomach to the wise old man.

Quickly, he lifted his shirt. There was a black mole on top of his belly button. The old man could not believe his eyes as he continued to stare at Abdullah Ibn Uthman. As his eyes remained fixed on the mole, the old man shouted: "I swear by the Lord of the Ka'ba that you are the one! "

Suddenly, there was complete silence in the room. The old man was preoccupied with the satisfaction of the confirmation of his knowledge while Abu Bakr felt quite timid about the fact that his virtuous character had been unveiled. The words of the old man were quite similar to those he had heard from the monk on the road to Damascus and Priest Bahira of Busra. It was the old man who again disrupted the silence: "I wish to warn you about an issue, so that you may refrain from it!"

The sincerity of the conversation had formed a warm, friendly atmosphere. It was as if the two men had known each other for ages. It was experience talking now, and Abu Bakr had to listen. He asked: "What will you warn me about?" By now, the old man was feeling more comfortable as he replied: "Do not give in to temptations…" Then he looked deep into Abu Bakr's eyes and continued, "Stay on the middle path of the righteous. Fear God and appreciate the blessings bestowed upon you."

Abu Bakr was on the right path anyway. He had learned to refrain from temptations at a very young age. He lived a disciplined life. However, this new information suggested that he had to be more cautious from that point on. Being a close friend to the Messenger of God, whose arrival was mentioned by the previous Prophets and many scholars, would not be easy. Obviously, this was a great blessing that could not be taken for granted. It had to be appreciated and carried with great sensitivity. A noble duty such as this could not be fulfilled in an environment where temptations and ego prevailed.

The middle path was the path of the prophets, and those that stood by their side had to remain on this path. It was imperative that they had the fear of God in their hearts and realized the blessings bestowed upon them could have easily been taken away. There was also the possibility that worldly ranks and wealth were given to test the level of Loyalty.

Finally, the meeting had concluded, and Abu Bakr left to attend to his business dealings. However, there were a million questions going through his mind. He was desperately trying to absorb all the confounding information he had heard. Something inside of him was persuading him to visit the old man again. Such an opportunity did not come by all the time. Upon completion of his business, he went back to the old man whom he considered as a precious source of information. The wise old man was pleased to see him again. He said: "I would like to give you these poems that I have written about the awaited Prophet."

Abu Bakr took the poems and placed them next to the one's he had written himself. According to the wise old man, the address was quite evident. Abu Bakr combined all the information he had heard previously with those explained by the old man. He realized that all roads led to Mecca, and all divinations pointed to his closest friend, Muhammad the Trustworthy.

At that particular instant, there was no one on earth more content than Abu Bakr. His trip to Yemen had earned him more profits than he had previously assumed.

At last, it was time to return to Mecca. Throughout the journey, his mind was preoccupied with the information he heard from the old man. He could not wait to share this information with Waraqa Ibn Nawfal. These thoughts had quite an influence on his walking tempo. The distance between Yemen and Mecca had never been so long for Abu Bakr.

Meanwhile in the cave of Hira, Muhammad the beloved servant of God had an inimitable experience. The divine union had occurred. The last Prophet of God and the Messenger awaited by those who possessed profundity had arrived. Muhammad returned to Mecca with the sanctified mission of inviting people to the right path. His mission was to convey the message of God brought by Gabriel, the angel who carried the divine revelations. Unfortunately, the Meccans' reaction to the new developments was not so welcoming.

Heading Towards the Communion

Abu Bakr was only a few hours from Mecca which had been shaken by the recent news. On his way to Mecca, he noticed a group of people who seemed to be waiting for something. As he came closer, he realized that the group consisted of prominent leaders of the Quraysh. Amongst them, there were renowned individuals such as Uqba Ibn Abi Muayt, Shayba, Rabia, Abu Jahl, and Abu'l Bahtare. This gathering was not a good sign. It was obvious that something had happened during his absence from Mecca. In a curious manner, Abu Bakr asked: "What happened during my absence? Is there a new development?"

They had been waiting for this question all along. Therefore, they began to explain with hatred and contempt:

> Oh Abu Bakr, the news is incredible! Abu Talib's orphan believes that he is a prophet. If it wasn't for you, we would have finished him off by now. However, you are here now, and we are certain that you will find a solution.

Their remarks carried two possible meanings. Perhaps, they were suggesting that it was time for Abu Bakr to break his ties from this man who had began to act in a peculiar manner. On the other hand, they could have been asking Abu Bakr to figure out the real reason behind his closest friend's behavior.

In any case, there was a situation in Mecca, and the leaders believed that it had to be dealt with immediately. From Abu Bakr's perspective, this was an anticipated development. Suddenly, everything he had heard and the people he had spoken to flashed before his eyes like a film-strip. The words of Zaid Ibn Amr, Bahira the Christian Monk, and the wise old man from Yemen began to make sense now. They were all directed at the same individual.

How could a man who had never been dishonest about anything, throughout the forty years of his life produce lies on behalf of God? He was Muhammad the Trustworthy… Without doubt, the awaited time had come.

Abu Bakr calmed the group down and assured them he would immediately look into the matter. Abu Bakr was a respected man, and they trusted him with the issue. For this reason, they agreed not to take any further action. Perhaps, they wanted to stay away from an issue that could have formed confusion in their own minds.

There was no time to waste; Abu Bakr quickly decided to visit Waraqa Ibn Nawfal. He was rushing through to streets of Mecca as he walked towards the house of Khadija. Destiny had placed him on this path, and no one could change his determined mind anymore.

After a short time, he was standing in front of Khadija's house. Quickly, he knocked on the door. The door was opened by the man he was looking for. How could there be a sign of deception on such face? The curiosity was eating Abu Bakr's mind away. However, he had to be certain. Initially, he stood distantly as he asked: "Oh Muhammad! Did you renounce the religion and tradition of your ancestors?"

Muhammad, peace and blessings be upon him, knew how to respond to a man who had been his closest friend for many years. He also knew Abu Bakr, inside-out. He replied, "Oh Abu Bakr, I am the Messenger of God!"

Then, he continued:

> God has sent me to you and to all of humanity, so that I will convey His message. I am inviting you to Him! Oh Abu Bakr, I swear by the Almighty, I am inviting you to the One and only true God. We serve no one but Him. Come and have faith in God!

Abu Bakr was treating the matter with extreme sensitivity. He wanted to be certain. Therefore, he asked: "What is your proof?"

The noble Messenger of God realized Abu Bakr's situation. He knew that Abu Bakr needed some sort of assurance. Perhaps, he needed some form of extraordinary evidence. Muhammad replied calmly: "The old man in Yemen."

Abu Bakr was stunned. Perhaps, he had heard about his trip to Yemen, but how could he have known about the old man? Was he aware of the conversation he had with the old man? Nevertheless, Abu Bakr had to be cautious. He regained his composure and said, "I spoke to many old men in Yemen."

This was an attempt to buy time as he needed to think about the entire issue. However, he was dealing with a blessed guide who possessed knowledge about a person's pulse. The noble Prophet wished to solve the matter as quickly as possible. Once again, with certainty, he replied: "The old man who gave you the poems!"

One could not look for a bigger proof. All the energy had been drained out of Abu Bakr. He had nothing else to say. All he could say was, "Who told you this, my beloved friend?" The noble Messenger replied: "The great angel who also came to those before I..."

There was only one thing left for Abu Bakr, and that was to grab the Prophet by the hand. With total sincerity and submission, he said: "Give me your hand, I wish to make my pledge to you."

Then with an emotional tone of voice, Abu Bakr declared the inundation of his soul: "I testify that there is no god but God and that Muhammad is his servant and Messenger."[22]

Indeed, Abu Bakr had submitted himself! This was a submission that would never be broken again. He became so emotional that he began to weep like a person who had found something he had lost a long time ago.

These were tears of joy, and Abu Bakr was not the only person shedding them. No one could feel more joy than the noble Messenger. Following Khadija, the rose of his house, his emancipated servant, Zaid Ibn Harith, and his uncle's son, Ali, another beloved soul had come before him to embrace his faith.

---

[22] Abu Ja'far et-Tabari, *er-Riyadu'n-Nadera*, 1/415

Abu Bakr was a man who had been going through the motion of preparation for so long. On that particular day, he made his decision so rapidly and without any hesitation that the noble Prophet described his inclusion to Islam with admiration: "Besides Abu Bakr, everyone I had invited to Islam experienced a period of hesitation. Abu Bakr, on the other hand, accepted my invitation without any hesitation."[23]

---

[23] *Sahih Bukhari*, 4/1701 (4364)

THE PROFIT OF A LIFE TIME

A highly regarded business man such as Abu Bakr always took well calculated steps before he made decisions. He was a man who could not risk his status in the world of the trade business. In those days, embracing Islam and supporting the Prophet meant confronting the entire world, beginning with Mecca. However, Abu Bakr represented a loyalty that would choose the side of the noble Prophet over the entire world. He knew that although he would face great difficulties and deficit due to his decision at the time, his reward would be enormous in the future. At the same time, when others preferred to go the other way, his devotion would earn him a unique rank that would be acknowledged beyond the heavens above.

Moreover, God was promising those who paid dues on his path, would be rewarded both in this life and in the life after death.[24] Was there a business deal more profitable than earning the pleasure of God and setting sail towards His infinite mercy? The choice made by Abu Bakr was a great indication of his brilliant mind in relation to business; he aimed to make the greatest profit with minimum risk involved.

---

[24] *Qur'an*, Ali Imran, 3/148

UTILIZING HIS SOCIAL STATUS

Following his acceptance of Islam, Abu Bakr began to utilize his reputation in the business world and in society to invite many of his friends to Islam. A significant number of people recognized Islam through Abu Bakr, may God be pleased with him. Each time he visited the Prophet, he would have one of his friends with him. Amongst them, there were important names such as Uthman Ibn Affan, Talha Ibn Ubaydullah, Abdurrahman Ibn Awf, Zubayr Ibn Awwam, and Sa'd Ibn Abi Waqqas. Each of these prominent personalities found serenity through the hands of Abu Bakr.

Abu Bakr himself had also found true peace by the side of the Messenger of God. For this reason, he wished to share this unique tranquility with others. He was ready to use all means in order to achieve this. For this divine cause, he was willing to place his wealth and life on the line. Abu Bakr knew that wealth spent on this path and life sacrificed for this cause would bring eternal qualities. Essentially, faith brought responsibility into the hearts it entered. Therefore, Abu Bakr was not going to be totally satisfied until others also benefitted from this source of spiritual nourishment.

At first, he tried to use his reputation and social status to invite people to Islam. Individuals such as Bilal and Ammar were poor, so the Quraysh would not even listen to them. However, Abu Bakr was a reputable leader. He began by inviting the wealthy and prominent personalities of Mecca to Islam. The mutual respect that existed between them had not been broken yet, so Abu Bakr used every opportunity to talk to them about God and His Messenger. His efforts had produced its fruits and five of the renowned companions, who were also in the group of ten men who had been given the glad tidings of paradise, came and embraced Islam. They were important individuals who had the potential of influencing hundreds of people around them. Time would confirm that through the hands of Abu Bakr, God would bring many significant individuals to His beloved messenger. These people would be the spiritual architects of the future.

ABU BAKR HELPS THE POOR

Abu Bakr had found his true path. He would never leave the side of the God's Prophet anymore. It was as if he had become his hands and feet. He was a soft-hearted man, and for this reason, he could not stand around and do nothing while the poor were being tortured because of their faith and beliefs. A man like Abu Bakr could not neglect the poor and the weak. Whenever the opportunity arose, he would run to their aid. He tried desperately to emancipate the slaves and to help those who were in need.

No one could compete with Abu Bakr in this sense. He was the champion of emancipation. One day, he heard a distressing scream that echoed through Mecca. He stopped and turned towards the direction where the sound was coming from. These were the screams of Bilal, who was being tortured. "One…One!" he shouted as he tried to put up a resistance. Abu Bakr rushed towards the direction of the sound. Then he came face to face with a horrific scene. Initially, he said: "Look at this poor man… have you no fear of God?" Then he continued: "What do you aim to achieve by this?" The tyrants, who had no shame, tried to blame Abu Bakr by arguing: "Aren't you the one who brainwashed him? Then, come and save him!"

This was a great opportunity for Abu Bakr. He accepted their offer and proposed an exchange. Abu Bakr had a servant who worshipped the idols. He offered him in exchange for Bilal. Umayya had tried every possible means to put some sense into his slave, Bilal. Luckily, he had failed. It was obvious that he had enough of dealing with Bilal so he accepted Abu Bakr's offer without any hesitation.

The agreement meant Bilal would be rescued from torture. Moreover, he was placed on a path that led to freedom. Abu Bakr's intention was not to purchase a slave but to provide Bilal with an opportunity to become a devoted Muslim by the side of the Messenger of God. By the testimony of Umar Ibn al-Khattab, Abu Bakr was a master who had liberated another master.[25]

On another occasion, he heard that a slave woman was being tortured simply because she had embraced Islam. Quickly, he went to the place where the incident had occurred. It was an abysmal scene. She had been beaten up so sadistically that her eyes were swollen. She had lost her vision in one of her eyes. Her young child sat in a curled up position at the corner, horrified by the entire ordeal. The little girl had lost her voice and sat crying silently. Could the heart of any human being endure such a grisly scene? Quickly, he purchased the woman and her little child from the monsters that had human appearances.

---

[25] Shaybane, *el-Ahad Wa'l-Mesane*, 1/202 (260)

Then without wasting a minute or asking for something in return, he emancipated the mother and her daughter.[26]

Abu Bakr rescued seven other slaves from such torture and gave them something they could not even dream of... their freedom.

Abu Bakr's father, Abu Kuhafa had noticed the unusual behavior of his son. He could not give any meaning to it, so he decided to caution him:

> My dear son, I have no objection to the emancipation of the slaves you purchase. However, shouldn't you choose the strong ones so that they could defend you against possible dangers that may come from the idol worshippers?

Abu Kuhafa had a rational argument. If Abu Bakr felt compelled to help those who were in need, he could have at least selected people who would be beneficial to him. This way, he would be getting something in return for his generosity.

However, this was Abu Bakr. Cheap concepts such as these had no value in his world. For those whose vision was limited by the boundaries of this world, being generous with an intention to gain a benefit was quite logical. But for those whose eyes were fixed on the pleasure of God, this was the greatest investment that one could ever make for the future. However, Abu Bakr had no intention of making an investment. According to him, this was a

---

[26] Abu Ja'far et-Tabari, *er-Riyadu'n-Nadera*, 2/22 (424)

form of gratitude and an appreciation for the wealth which was bestowed upon him. His reply to his insistent father was very meaningful: "My beloved father! Without doubt, I am not doing this to gain a benefit but to earn the endorsement of God!"[27]

Of course, father Kuhafa was not aware of the fact that the Messenger of God approved of his son's actions and character. On one occasion, the Prophet stated that no one amongst his community could be more compassionate toward them than Abu Bakr.[28]

A person who only sought the pleasure God was also complimented by the heavens and beyond. Shortly thereafter, verses praising the efforts and munificence of those who were on this holy path were revealed, with Abu Bakr being on top of the list. The holy Qur'an promised an eternal world of luminosity to those who lived in fear of God as well as those who constantly thought about others, gave generously, testified to the truth, and sought after righteousness.[29]

---

[27] Hakim, *Mustadrak*, 2/572 (3942)
[28] *Sunanu't-Tirmidhi*, 5/664 (3790)
[29] Layl, 92:5-7

RACE TO SERVE HUMANITY

Abu Bakr chased every opportunity to serve the values in which he had total faith. He wanted to utilize his experience and wisdom solely on this path. Abu Bakr possessed a deep knowledge in genealogy. He made the most of his knowledge by providing information to the noble Messenger about people who visited Mecca to gather information about Islam. This gave the Prophet a prior knowledge about the people he confronted. The information supplied by Abu Bakr helped those who came to the Prophet understand Islam better and made it easier for them to become Muslims.

In those days such behavior was unacceptable in Mecca. One after another, the wealthy and the noble were embracing Islam. At the same time, the poor received support, and slaves became emancipated. Mecca was under siege from two directions. On the one side, it was losing its wealthy citizens to Islam, and on the other, the city was becoming deprived of its servants and slaves.

The Quraysh could not sit back and watch Abu Bakr manipulate their men, and they did not. Before long, they began to approach Abu Bakr with hostility. The Quraysh could not tolerate the open invitation made by Abu Bakr any longer. Abu Bakr had begun to recite the Qur'an and to perform his prayers in public. The changes in his character were noticed by everyone who neared him and listened to the recitation. In amazement, they watched him recite the Qur'an as tears flowed from his eyes.

The non-believers had no sympathy as they began a violent campaign against their friends with whom they had dined and drank together not long before. They had one objective, and that was to eliminate the people who they had declared as the common enemy. Each passing day, the dosage of violence and animosity towards believers drastically increased. At this point in history, the number of Muslims had not yet reached forty. Abu Bakr insisted on inviting people to Islam openly and in public. He asked for the Prophet's permission to do this. At first, the noble Messenger explained the significant difference in the balance of power. Then he said: "We are but a few men!" However, he did not wish to break Abu Bakr's heart, so together they came to the Ka'ba. Abu Bakr began to explain Islam as a crowd slowly gathered around him. This also gave Abu Bakr the honor of being the first orator of Islam.

The Quraysh had no tolerance for new developments in the community unless they were endorsed by them. Suddenly, a group of thugs attacked Abu Bakr. They mercilessly hit everyone who stood in their way with whatever they could grab. Abu Bakr was the main target. They had managed to knock him to the ground and kicked him while he tried desperately to protect his head. Utba Ibn Rabia was the main culprit. He possessed so much enmity towards Abu Bakr that he wanted to kick him until he was dead. Abu Bakr's face was covered in blood. They had broken his nose. Abu Bakr was in no condition to put up a resistance anymore. As his motionless body lay on the ground, finally, they walked away, assuming that Abu Bakr was dead.

Abu Bakr's relatives had rushed to the scene. Quickly, they picked up his unconscious body and carried him home. Realizing the seriousness of his condition, a group of his relatives returned to the Ka'ba and shouted: "By God! If Abu Bakr dies, we will kill Utba!"

All of his relatives had gathered at Abu Bakr's house. They were trying desperately to revive him. They were asking him to speak. They wanted to know if he was still alive.

A few hours later, Abu Bakr began to show signs of life as he tried to move his body. Abu Bakr was alive indeed. Everyone showed a sigh of relief. This incident could have triggered a blood-feud which, in turn, may have continued for many years.

Abu Bakr had a purpose in life, and he was well aware of this. Nothing but His love inhabited Abu Bakr's heart. He had been prepared for days like this from the beginning when he had decided to place his wealth and life on the line for the Messenger of God. He tried to regain his composure, but it was impossible to stand up. He attempted to say something, and his lips were trembling as he muttered: "Is the Messenger of God, all right?"

This was impossible for them to comprehend. A man who had almost died had finally regained consciousness and was asking about the well-being of another. They took no notice of it as they tried to feed him. Little did they know that his nourishment did not come from food. How could Abu Bakr eat when he had no news of the Prophet's safety? He could not even take a sip of cold water unless he was assured of the Prophet's well-being.

His relatives left the house knowing that Abu Bakr was feeling better now. He was left alone with his beloved mother. As Abu Bakr opened his eyes again, his mother stood there with a bowl of soup in her hand. Once again, Abu Bakr asked in anxiety: "How is the Messenger of God? Is he all right?"

Abu Bakr's mother replied with a confused expression on her face: "By God, I have no knowledge of your master!"

As a mother, her heart was burning with sorrow. This was the son she begged for from God for so many years. Now he was lying before her, covered in blood.

Abu Bakr tried frantically to stand up, but he could not manage to come to his feet. Therefore, he begged his mother; "Please mother! Can you go to Ummu Jamil, the daughter of Khattab and find out what happened to him?"

The compassionate heart of a mother could not refuse the request of her son. Quickly, she went to Ummu Jamil. In desperation, she asked: "Abu Bakr is asking about the condition of Muhammad, the son of Abdullah."

However, these were the days in which people refrained from announcing their faith. Ummu Jamil had also embraced Islam, but she feared the wrath of the Quraysh.

Initially, she said that she knew nothing about Muhammad or Abu Bakr. Then she realized that there was an urgency about the entire issue. Abu Bakr's mother would not come all the way to her door unless there was a serious problem. Then she said, "There is something strange about this..."

She stepped out with Ummu'l Khayr and came to Abu Bakr. She could not hold her feelings back upon seeing Abu Bakr in that condition. She neglected the whole issue of concealing her faith when she screamed: "Only the people of rebellion would do this to you! I pray that God will take revenge for what they have done to you."

Abu Bakr's reaction was the same: "Is the Messenger of God all right?"

Suddenly, she realized that she had said too much. She decided to be more cautious and replied: "Your mother is in the room, she can hear us."

Abu Bakr had total confidence in his mother. He said: "Do not be alarmed, no harm will come to you from her. She can keep a secret."

This was enough for Ummu Jamil, and she gave Abu Bakr the news he had been waiting for: "He is alive and well!"

It was obvious that Abu Bakr would not be satisfied by this. He was a symbol of Loyalty. Once again, he asked: "Where is he now?"

"At Arqam's house, she replied."

Abu Bakr's pain would not go away until he had laid eyes upon the Prophet. He had to see him with his own eyes. As he tried to stand up, he said: "I swear by the

Almighty, I will not eat a morsel of food or drink a drop of water until I see him with my own eyes."

There was no other option but to take Abu Bakr to the Prophet of God. They waited until nightfall, when things had calmed down. Then they helped Abu Bakr walk towards the house of Arqam.

As he walked through the door, he came face to face with the Messenger of God. Then Abu Bakr, the symbol of Loyalty began to kiss the Prophet's radiant face and eyes. He was in a terrible condition, yet he was behaving as if they had given him the world. He was feeling a sense of contentment which could not be described with words. Abu Bakr loved the Prophet more than his own mother and father. Nevertheless, God's Messenger stated that if we were to choose a friend from among his community, it would be Abu Bakr.[30]

At this point, all the companions who were present began to weep when they saw Abu Bakr's wounds. The atmosphere had become so emotional that even the Prophet could not hold his emotions back anymore. Abu Bakr noticed the Prophet's sorrow. He could not stand there and watch the Prophet feel sad because of what had happened to him. Abu Bakr was a sensitive man. Immediately, he took control over his own emotions and said: "Oh noble Messenger of God, I would sacrifice my parents for you. Do not be concerned for me. I am all right. The only pain I feel is on my face, where the non-believer kicked."

---

[30] *Sahih Muslim*, 1/67 (44)

What kind of a love was this? He was feeling an additional sorrow because of the fact that his pain had saddened the Prophet. He was trying desperately to convince the Prophet that he was feeling better. He felt so close to the Messenger of God, peace and blessings be upon him, that he did not wish to waste the opportunity to do something for his mother. He pointed at Ummu Khayr, and with a broken voice, he said:

> Oh noble Messenger of God, this is my mother! She possesses a deep love for me and respects her own parents. You are a sanctified soul. Can you please invite her to God? Offer a prayer for her so that God protects her from hellfire.

Abu Bakr displayed a tremendous sincerity in this moment. His moral fiber represented the notion of self-sacrifice. How could the Messenger of God decline such a heartfelt request? He raised his hands and prayed to his Merciful Lord. He beseeched that the seed of faith be planted in the heart of Abu Bakr's beloved mother.

Perhaps, it was the right moment for the greatest blessing. Abu Bakr's mother, Ummu Khayr embraced Islam, there and then.[31]

Abu Bakr had come face to face with death only a few hours ago, and now he was feeling extremely joyful. Even at times like these, he was concerned with the salvation of others. His mother's conversion had removed all of his

---

[31] Ibn Hajar, *el-Isaba*, 8/200 (12006)

suffering. He spent the next month at the house of al Arqam by the side of the noble Messenger.

At the time, there were thirty-nine of them. The Prophet's uncle Hamza also embraced Islam on the day that Abu Bakr was almost beaten to death.[32]

One day, the noble Messenger went to the Ka'ba. Once again, he was confronted by the Quraysh. Immediately, they began to harass the Prophet: "Oh Muhammad! Are you the one who forbids us from worshipping the gods of our ancestors?"

"Yes, I am the one," replied the Prophet."

This was enough of a reason for them. They attacked him like a pack of hungry wolves. They were pestering a savior who tried desperately to pull them out of the darkness of falsehood. Uqba Ibn Abi Muayt had wrapped his turban around the Prophet's neck. He was trying to suffocate him to death. Abu Bakr was appalled by the entire incident, and he quickly pounced on Uqba. At the same time, he tried frantically to keep the rest of the thugs away from the Prophet. Like the believer from the family of the Pharaoh mentioned in the Qur'an, Abu Bakr shouted: "Are you going to kill a man because he says God is my Lord!"[33]

Indeed, it was illogical to rebel against a man who was sent by the Almighty himself. He had come with eternal messages and performed miracles. No one was forcing them to believe; they had the choice of following their

---

[32] Hayseme, *Majmau'z-Zawaed*, 9/267
[33] *Sahih ibn Hebban*, 14/526; *Qur'an*, Mumin 40:28

own paths and beliefs. However, if they wished to accept his invitation, they would have earned the honor of walking towards eternal paradise together. The path to salvation was being offered to them, and it was their choice to accept or decline.

Whenever and wherever righteousness and the message of God were conveyed, there were always those who opposed it. Because of this, there was also a need for people like Abu Bakr, who defend their beloved at all cost and with tears in their eyes.

That evening when Abu Bakr returned home, he noticed a wound on his head. He had not felt it during the chaos of the moment. One of the non-believers must have caused the injury when he had grabbed him by the hair.

Many years later, during the Caliphate of Ali, a conversation took them back to the early days. Ali asked those who were present at the gathering: "Oh People! Who is the most courageous and valiant of all human beings?" They replied without any hesitation, "It is you, the leader of believers!"

Upon hearing their reply, Ali shook his head from side to side and then he said: "When I confront the enemy, I always do my best to finish him off. However, Abu Bakr is the true possessor of courage." Following his statement, Ali fixed his eyes on the horizon and continued:

One day, we raised a tent, and we were discussing the matter of who should protect the Prophet from a possible ambush. By God, no one had volunteered yet when Abu

Bakr suddenly drew his sword and stood next to the Prophet. I swear by God, Abu Bakr was the bravest of us all.

Talking about unforgettable memories brought back even more memories. He also told them about the event we have previously mentioned where Abu Bakr said: "Are you going to kill a man because he says God is my Lord!"

As Ali explained his memories, he became so emotional that words got stuck in his throat. He was sobbing and talking at the same time. Frequently, he used a handkerchief to cover his face as he tried desperately to conceal his grief, but his beard was drenched in tears. This was clear sign of his emotional state. Before long, everyone at the gathering began to weep. After a while, Ali regained his composure and asked: "Now tell me, who's more hallowed, the believer from the Pharaoh's family or Abu Bakr?"

This elite group realized what followed. As they pondered the answer, they began to weep again. They were crying so passionately that no one had the energy to answer the question. Realizing this, Ali decided to answer his own question:

> I swear by the Almighty! Being with Abu Bakr is more blessed than anything on earth, including the believer from the Pharaoh's family because the believer from the Pharaoh's family concealed his faith while Abu Bakr announced his publicly.[34]

---

[34] Hayseme, *Majmau'z-Zawaed*, 9/47

JOURNEY TOWARDS THE LAND OF ABYSSINIA

Mecca had become a dangerous place for the believers. Moreover, there was positive feedback from the group that migrated to Abyssinia (Ethiopia). Soon, Abu Bakr also asked for permission to migrate to Abyssinia. The request was rational, so the Prophet granted permission. The harassments and violence against Muslims had increased drastically in Mecca, but the world was a big place. So Abu Bakr left Mecca with his cousin. They were heading towards the land of Abyssinia. Abu Bakr was happy because would be reunited with the companions who had migrated to Abyssinia before him. Muslims in Abyssinia were practicing their religion freely and worshipping their Lord the way it was taught by the Prophet. Abu Bakr was also feeling joyful about the fact that he would get the opportunity to practice his religion openly.

A short while later, they came across Ibn Dugunna, a man respected by all of Mecca. He was one of Abu Bakr's oldest friends. He was surprised to see Abu Bakr on the road, as he asked curiously: "Where are you going?"

Abu Bakr replied: "My clan forced me out of my home land. They harassed me and imposed financial sanctions on me."

Ibn Dugunna was in shock. How could someone like Abu Bakr be forced into such situation? He was a virtuous man who possessed a wonderful heart and a kind nature that embraced everyone in the community. Ibn Dugunna asked with confusion: "Why would they do this to you?" Then he continued, "I swear by God, you surpass all of us in regards to supporting those close to you, helping those who are in need, and looking after the poor. Turn back at once. From this point on, you are under my protection."

Abu Bakr had left his heart behind at Mecca anyway; how could he tolerate a life of exodus while his beloved master remained in Mecca. A man like Abu Bakr had to return and take his place by the Prophet's side. This was the type of behavior expected from a man of unique Loyalty. Ibn Dugunna's offer was a historical proposal that he could not ignore. Therefore, he accepted it with great joy.

So, they returned to Mecca together with Ibn Dugunna. Immediately, after entering Mecca, Ibn Dugunna grabbed Abu Bakr by the hand and took him to the Ka'ba. Then he shouted at the large crowd that had gathered there: "Oh the people of the Quraysh! I have taken the son of Abu Kuhafa under my wings! From this day on, let no man approach him with hostility!" The Quraysh did not wish to disappoint Ibn Dugunna. However, they had a condition. Abu Bakr would not be allowed to perform his prayers in public, and he would be banned from inviting people to Islam.

Abu Bakr designated a corner outside of his house for worshipping his Lord. Here, he performed his daily prayers and recited the Qur'an with his velvety voice. In tears, he begged for the mercy of his Lord. Abu Bakr's sincerity and devotion was attracting many people who came regularly just to watch him perform the prayers and listen to him as he recited the Qur'an. His house had become a gathering point for slaves, women, and children.

Invitation through practice was the most effective method of winning the hearts of human beings. Abu Bakr was achieving this without realization. However, it did not take long for the Quraysh to realize the apparent changes in people. Quickly, they came to Ibn Dugunna and argued:

> "Without doubt you are not protecting Abu Bakr so that he could be a burden upon us. However, as he performs his prayers and recites the Qur'an, he is displaying such exemplary manner that we fear our children and women will convert to Islam."

In saying this, they did not even realize that they were confirming the beauty of Abu Bakr's faith. Unfortunately, obstinacy and superstition was a huge barrier that prevented them from reaching out to this evident beauty. The thing that threatened them the most was the fact that their false beliefs had no chance against the divine truth. They were hiding from reality and wanted to conceal their weaknesses from others. A short while after, they came back to Ibn Dugunna and said: "Go and tell him to stay in his house. He may do whatever he wishes in the privacy of his own home."

They were requesting that Abu Bakr perform his prayers and recite the Qur'an in private. Ibn Dugunna was influenced by the persistent attitude of the Quraysh. He came to Abu Bakr and said: "I did not take you under my protection so that you could be a burden to these people. You are disturbing them. Go into to your house and perform your worship there." For Abu Bakr, living under the protection of a non-believer, whose condition was that he be banned from inviting people to Islam, reciting the Qur'an, and performing his daily prayers out in the open, was not an honorable thing. In such a situation, the only honorable thing to do was to take refuge in the mercy of God. His current situation reminded you of a caged lion. Humanity needed his services. Therefore, Abu Bakr had to break his chains and attend to his duties no matter what the consequences were. He began to weigh his options. If he abided by their rules, he would have no problems with practicing his religion at home. However, the fundamentals of his faith suggested this was not a religion of individualism. Otherwise, why would the noble Prophet tolerate such anguish? Along with personal responsibilities, it was an obligation to hold others by the hand and bring them face to face with the divine truth. Thus, a man like Abu Bakr did what he was supposed to do. He went to Ibn Dugunna and told him that he was removing himself

Journey Towards the Land of Abyssinia 57

from his protection. He declared that he had taken refuge in the mercy of God.[35]

Unfortunately, in those days such declaration was considered an invitation to trouble. Abu Bakr had broken through the chains of restriction. From that day on, he tried to fulfill his religious obligations at the Ka'ba. However, this was not an easy task. The Quraysh considered this as a deliberate provocation. They were outraged by Abu Bakr's attitude. Something had to be done, so they decided to follow him with every step he took.

One day, Abu Bakr was performing his prayer at the Ka'ba. One of the thugs of the Quraysh grabbed a handful of dirt from the ground, walked up to him, and then hurled the dirt on the prostrating head of Abu Bakr as he shouted words of insult. As Abu Bakr tried to wipe the dirt off his body, he came face to face with one of the chieftains of Mecca who took a glance deep into his eyes.[36]

Did Abu Bakr's actions cause any harm to anyone? Who could endorse or justify such harassment? Hoping a glimmer of humanity remained in this person, Abu Bakr said: "Look what this thug has done to me!" Unfortunately, this person did not possess a sensible bone in his body, and he replied: "You brought this upon yourself!"

He was implying that by taking himself out of Ibn Dugunna's protection, Abu Bakr had sent an invitation to

---

[35] *Sahih Bukhari*, 2/804 (2175)
[36] Reports suggest that this person was either As ibn Wael or Waleed Ibn'ul-Mugira

the thugs of Mecca. Perhaps there was nothing else to say. These were the remarks of a heedless man. Abu Bakr had no other option but to beseech the mercy and aid of his Lord. He raised his hands and began to implore: "You are the All-Merciful! You are the All-Merciful! You are the All-Merciful![37]"

Abu Bakr's prayer described the immense mercy of God, Who showed great patience against the hoodlums who were in the habit of presenting the night as day and black as white. Abu Bakr displayed his amazement at God's mercy that embraced even those who rebelled against Him.

---

[37] Ibn Hisham, *es-Siratu'n-Nabawiyyah*, 2/218

THE BOYCOTT

The rancor possessed by the Quraysh did not ease with time. On the contrary, their rage increased with each passing day. They sent an envoy to Abyssinia. A group of men with precious gifts asked the King of Abyssinia to release the Muslim refugees into their custody. However, their attempts had failed and the king had refused their request. They returned to Mecca empty-handed. This was a bad sign for the Quraysh; it meant that Muslims had found a nation, where they could seek refuge and practice their faith freely. The Quraysh were constantly losing their authority over the Muslims. Harassing and insulting the weak and the poor was not going to be so easy anymore.

Moreover, powerful figures such as Hamza and Umar Ibn al-Khattab had also embraced Islam. The leaders of the Quraysh gathered at a crisis meeting to find a solution to the changing conditions. Finally, they came to an agreement to impose sanctions against the believers. They would cut all ties with them and suspend all business dealings. Even the simplest things such as selling food to Muslims would be banned. The believers were exiled from Mecca into a nearby location in the desert.

They were left to die there during the boycott that lasted for three long years.

Abu Bakr was amongst those who were banished from Mecca. Abu Talib's compassionate soul had prevailed, and he designated his land to all those who were expelled from Mecca. They raised tents with whatever they found and strived to survive in the desert.

These years of despair would be quite challenging. Famine and ailments took control over the exiled community. The tragic screams of people enduring the pain of starvation or illness could be heard almost every single day. Abu Bakr was one of the leading individuals who tried desperately to help these people with whatever he owned.

The three years of anguish passed under the dark clouds of pain and suffering. However, there was more tragedy yet to come. The Prophet's greatest protector, Abu Talib passed away. As the Prophet mourned the death of his uncle, his beloved wife Khadija the Pure also passed away. These were the years of sadness and despair…

THE TRUTHFUL ONE

Finally, the night in which the Almighty honored His Prophet with Isra and Miraj (the night journey and the Ascension) arrived. With this, the Omnipotent God manifested that He was behind His Prophet, no matter what kind of challenge or difficulty he faced. Within a short period of time, he had traveled an unimaginable distance and returned with incredible knowledge about this world and the hereafter. Years were squeezed into seconds in which the Prophet was blessed with an abundance of divine compliments.

The following day, this incredible journey was the talk of the town. The Meccans were making fun of it and ridiculing the Prophet's claim. As Abu Jahl passed by the Ka'ba, he noticed a group of men gathered around the Prophet. He approached the group and with a teasing manner, he asked: "What is the latest news? What happened last night?" The Messenger of God, peace and blessings be upon him, turned his face towards Abu Jahl and replied calmly: "Last night, my Lord took me to Bayt al-Maqdis (in Jerusalem)."

Abu Jahl was confused as he asked: "Then you returned back to Mecca?" They were aware of the fact that such challenging journey took many months to complete. Abu

Jahl was being quite sarcastic with this line of questioning. The Prophet replied without hesitation: "Yes, I performed a prayer with my brothers, the previous Prophets."

Upon hearing this, Abu Jahl screamed with joy. This was a great opportunity for him. Finally, he could prove the Prophet wrong. With a soft tone of voice, he asked: "If I gather my clan here, would you explain this to them?"

There was no reason to conceal the incident. This was a great gift bestowed upon the Prophet by his Lord. People had to be informed; therefore, the Prophet agreed to do it. Abu Jahl became extremely blissful as he had the word of Muhammad. Quickly, he began to shout: "Oh the sons of Ka'b! Come here quickly!"

By now, everyone had heard of Muhammad's extraordinary claim. Quickly, they went to Abu Bakr. They were certain that once Abu Bakr heard this claim, his path with Muhammad the Trustworthy would part forever. They believed that this was the end of Muhammad. As soon as Abu Bakr opened the door, they said: "Oh Ateeq! What your friend has told us until this day was rational to a certain degree, and they were uncomplicated things. However, come and listen to the claim he is making today!"

Abu Bakr was a soft man, and he feared that something had happened to his master. In panic, he asked: "Shame on you! What have you done to him!" They stared at Abu Bakr with cynical eyes and replied: "He is at the Ka'ba now, telling people how he traveled to Bayt al-Maqdis last night."

Another person quickly intervened and said, "He claims that he came back the same night!" Abu Bakr glanced at them with a pitiful expression on his face and then replied: "Oh people! What is wrong with that?" He wished to touch on their emotions as he continued, "I have belief in things beyond this. I believe that he receives information from heavens and beyond, throughout the day and the night. I verify this!"

They had come to Abu Bakr's door hoping to confuse him about the genuineness of his friend, and they were certain such claim would have broken the ties between Abu Bakr and Muhammad. But now, they were shocked by Abu Bakr's remarks. They all swallowed their pride along with their enthusiasm as Abu Bakr made the final historical statement; "If Muhammad has indeed claimed this, then it must be the truth!"[38]

These were the extraordinary words of Abu Bakr. He had not learned them from his ancestors. For Abu Bakr, authenticity of a statement was not measured according to what the people of the Hejaz claimed but according to the words of Muhammad, who was the architect of his mind and soul. This is why he did not even think about asking questions like, "are you sure that you heard correctly" or "was it really he who made this claim." Abu Bakr did not even display the slightest of doubt on his face. This was a great disappointment for the non-believers. With this statement, Abu Bakr had earned the title of "the truthful

---

[38] Abu Ja'far et-Tabari, *er-Riyadu'n-Nadrate*, 1/403 (322)

one." From that day on, he would be known as the Siddiq (the truthful one). Following his confrontation with the non-believers, Abu Bakr rushed to the Masjid and listened to the entire incident from the mouth of the Prophet. Once again, he made the same declaration before the Messenger of God. In reply, the noble Messenger said: "O Abu Bakr! You are a Siddiq (truthful one)!"[39]

---

[39] Abu Ja'far et-Tabari, *er-Riyadu'n-Nadrate*, 1/403 (322)

THE HOLY MIGRATION AND THE SPIRIT OF COMPANIONSHIP

The Messenger of God was feeling so close to Abu Bakr that he visited him day and night. Meanwhile, the permission to migrate had been granted, and the holy migration to Medina had commenced. Just as those who migrated before him, Abu Bakr came to the Prophet and asked for permission to go. The noble Messenger said: "Do not rush! Perhaps God will grant you a friend."

Abu Bakr understood exactly what the Prophet was implying. He thanked his Lord for this peerless blessing. Then, he began to prepare for the important journey ahead. A short while later, Abu Bakr made all the necessary preparations. All he had to do now was to wait for the Prophet's command.

A few days after, the noble Messenger came to Abu Bakr's house at an unusual time of the day. Traditionally, house visits at midday were quite uncommon in this society; therefore, Abu Bakr realized that there was a new development. He waited patiently for the Messenger of God to speak. At first, the noble Prophet asked to speak in privacy. Abu Bakr replied restlessly: "Do not be alarmed, oh noble Messenger of God! They are my daughters. What has happened?" The noble Prophet replied swiftly: "Permission to migrate has been granted to me." Abu Bakr became extremely excited by the Prophet's reply, and he asked again: "Are we going together, oh noble Messenger of God?" The Prophet calmly answered: "Yes, together."

This was a decision that would change history. Once again, Abu Bakr was being blessed with the noble duty of accompanying the Prophet on the holy journey. Was there a greater blessing than this? Although, the signs were there and the Prophet had hinted this before, hearing it from the mouth of the God's Messenger gave Abu Bakr a different sense of joy. Abu Bakr became so emotional that he began to shed tears of joy.

Perhaps, many thoughts were crossing his mind at that very moment. The news he had heard from Waraqa Ibn Nawfal, glad tidings given by the old man from Yemen, and the predictions made by monk Bahira must have been the highlight of his memories. Divine destiny was about to occur. Just as those before him, the noble Messenger of God would also embark on a journey away from his homeland.

However, they needed to be extra careful because traveling with camels was not going to be easy. For this reason, they made a deal with a guide name Abdullah Ibn Uraykit. He was a polytheist from the Abd Ibn Adiyy clan.[40]

---

[40] Abu Ja'far et-Tabari, *er-Riyadu'n-Nadrate*, 1/403 (322)

This man had comprehensive knowledge about the region, and he could be trusted. Clearly, qualifications were important in such risky situations. The plans were made, and they planned to meet at Thawr in three days' time. Their guide would bring two camels to the meeting place. Abu Bakr had purchased these camels specifically for the journey.

Abu Bakr spoke to his daughter Asma and made sure that she visited them at Thawr. According to their plan, she would bring rations and news from Mecca. Her sister Aisha informs us that Asma concealed the food and drinks under her sash, where she made two separate compartments. Then she carried the goods to Thawr. For this reason, she was given the title of "Zunnitaqayn," owner of two sashes.[41]

Another precaution taken by Abu Bakr was the tactic he gave to his shepherd Amr, who cared for his sheep. He told Amr to follow them with the herd so that their tracks would be covered.[42]

Finally, the time had arrived. The noble Messenger stepped out of his home with Abu Bakr as the group of polytheists surrounded his house with a plan to assassinate him. The noble Messenger grabbed a handful of earth from the ground and hurled it on their faces as he recited a verse from the holy Qur'an. The assassins did not even see the Prophet as he walked pass them. The noble Mes-

---

[41] Az-Zar'e, *Zadu'l-Mead*, 3/52
[42] *Sahih Bukhari*, 3/1087 (2817)

senger knew that even if they left Mecca, they would not be given the right to life. Therefore, he had to take extreme measures. He planned to head towards the opposite direction to a high hill top called Thawr. Here, they would hide and watch the developments as they unfolded in Mecca.

Abu Bakr had to enter the cave first. He had great concerns for the safety of his beloved Prophet. He felt to need to check out the cave before the Prophet entered. He feared the Prophet could be bitten by a poisonous snake. Quickly, he tried to block all the gaps and the holes that were present on the walls of the cave. He was using whatever he could find, including a piece of fabric he had torn off from his own garment.

They stayed in the cave for three days. Abu Bakr was constantly on the lookout throughout their stay on the mountain. At the end of each day, as Meccans entered their homes to rest, Abu Bakr's son, Abdullah visited them, bringing new information from Mecca.

Meanwhile, in Mecca, the assassins had invaded the Prophet's home only to find young Ali sleeping on the Prophet's bed. They had let the Prophet slip away from their hands, and they were gnashing their teeth with rage. Muhammad had to be found. For this reason, they decided to place a bounty on his head. Dead or alive, they searched for him frantically. The Quraysh was keen to find Muhammad using every means available.

Abu Jahl possessed a witty mind. He came to Abu Bakr's house as soon as he heard the news of Muhammad's departure from Mecca. He began to interrogate Abu Bakr's daughter Asma. At first, he asked for the whereabouts of her father. Asma told him that she did not know, but Abu Jahl became extremely furious by her reply. With rage, he struck her on the face. Abu Jahl slapped her with so much power that it almost ripped Asma's earring off her ear. Under normal circumstances, such an insult towards a young girl would have been considered as a shameful act. However, this was Abu Jahl. When Asma remembered the incident, she would say: "That man is a filthy transgressor!"[43]

Meanwhile, expert trackers had followed their tracks all the way to Thawr. They climbed Thawr, looking for them. However, they failed to see the two friends who had God as their third companion. As the bounty hunters stood in front of the cave, they were so close that Abu Bakr could see their feet and hear their grunts. Abu Bakr became so nervous that the Prophet could clearly see the concern on his face. His only fear was for the safety of the Prophet. Once again, it was up to the noble Prophet to calm down his friend. Abu Bakr was a man whom the Prophet addressed as brother. He looked deep into Abu Bakr's eyes and calmly said: "Oh Abu Bakr! Why do you have concerns for the two who have God as the third?"[44]

This was the Messenger of God speaking. He revealed that God had informed him that He would protect His

---
[43] *Sahih Bukhari*, 3/1419 (3692)
[44] Abu Nuaym, *Hilyetu'l-Awliya*, 2/56

Messenger from all possible harm coming from human beings.[45] The Prophet was certain of this. He knew that God would help his last Messenger as he helped those before him. Without doubt, the Almighty would bring peace and serenity upon his Prophet and support him against the Quraysh. Finally, their pursuers had left; perhaps the rest of their journey would become considerably safer. Soon after, Amr arrived with their camels. He had also brought along their guide from the clan of Abdullah Ibn Adiyy.

Abu Bakr chose the healthiest camel and offered it to the Prophet: "May my mother and father be sacrificed for you! Get on your mount, oh noble Messenger of God!" However, the Prophet's reply was unexpected: "I will not mount a camel that does not belong to me!" Abu Bakr did not know what to do in a situation like this. He said: "Oh noble Messenger of God! The camel is yours!" Abu Bakr's offer did not solve the problem. The Prophet insisted: "I will not accept unless I pay the amount that you paid for the camel." Abu Bakr had no other alternative but to disclose the amount he had given for the camel. Then the Prophet said: "I have purchased this from you for the same amount." Even during this significant part of the holy pilgrimage, the noble Prophet was teaching his people a valuable lesson.

Then came the time when they left the cave to head towards their destination, Medina. The only people

---

[45] *Sahih Bukhari*, 3/1337 (3453)

accompanying the Prophet on this grueling journey were Abu Bakr and a guide who was a non-believer. Most of the bounty hunters had returned to Mecca empty-handed. However, there were a few who refused to give up on the handsome bounty offered for the Prophet's head.

As they made their way towards Medina, they noticed a cloud of dust approaching from a distance. Once again, Abu Bakr began to show signs of panic. Unlike the cave, this time they had no cover. Moreover, they had no weapons to protect themselves. Abu Bakr had great concern for the Prophet's life. In panic, he shouted: "Oh noble Messenger! He is catching up!" The noble Messenger invited Abu Bakr to serenity: "Do not fear, for God is with us!"

Certainly, no one could harm a person who was given a mission by God himself. Was there a safer place to take refuge than in the mercy of God? As the rider approached, they realized that it was Suraka. As Abu Bakr became quite edgy, the noble Prophet turned back and glanced at Suraka. It was obvious that the Prophet was trying to take Suraka under control with his powerful gaze. His intention was to pin the enemy down with his eyes.

It was a moment of divine submission. The Prophet's lips were in motion. He was praying to his Lord. Suddenly, the front legs of Suraka's horse sank into the sand. The animal had thrown its rider a few meters away. A cloud of dust rose from the spot where Suraka fell. He was also trapped in the sand.

At first, he assumed that this was an accident. However, the incident did not seem like an accident. What could have caused such a thing? There was no logical reason. Was Muhammad really the Prophet of God? What if what they said about him was true? Suraka thought about these possibilities for a brief moment. There was no other explanation. He stared at the Prophet for a short while and then said: "Pray to God for me so that He saves me from this! I give you my word... I will not pursue you anymore!"

Muhammad was the Messenger of God. How could he turn down such a request, even if it was coming from an enemy? The noble Messenger prayed, and Suraka stood up as if nothing had happened. For a brief moment, he thought about the handsome bounty. Then, quickly, he mounted his horse and attempted to advance towards the Prophet. Once again, the front legs of the horse sank into the sand. This time they went deeper into the ground. Suraka could not give any meaning to this. He had been riding through the desert for many years and had never encountered such an inexplicable event. He thought to himself, "Abu Jahl was wrong; it was Abu Bakr who spoke the truth!" It was quite clear that they were trying to harm the people who were under the protection of God. This time, he was quite sincere as he shouted from the top of his lungs:

> "Oh Muhammad! I realized that your prayers are the cause of these strange occurrences. I have camels at a certain location, take them, they are yours, but please

save me from this situation. I will definitely let you
go this time."

The Prophet's initial reply was: "I have no need for your camels." Then he prayed for Suraka. Once again, Suraka stood up with his horse.[46] A million thoughts must have crossed his mind as Suraka stood there covered in dust. This time, the radical change in his spiritual world was evident on his face. Abu Bakr was stunned by the entire incident as he thanked his Lord for protecting the noble Messenger, peace and blessings be upon him. Suraka was about to drop to his knees. The noble Messenger glanced at Suraka as if his expression carried the following message: "You too?" "Yes, oh noble Messenger of God! replied Suraka. Then he gave his word to Muhammad, peace and blessings be upon him. He said he would go back and distract all those who pursue the Prophet."[47]

In this situation, everyone needed to display their talents, and when it was necessary, sacrifices had to be made. Suraka had submitted to God, and he had to prove his loyalty by protecting the Messenger of God. Following the agreement, the noble Prophet said: "Oh Suraka, what will you do on the day that you put on the two bracelets of Chosroes."[48]

This was a triple blessing for Suraka. He was released without a ransom, blessed with Islam, and honored with

---

[46] *Sahih Ibn Hebban*, 14/190
[47] *Sahih Muslim*, 4/2309 (2009)
[48] Ibn Abdelbarr, *al-Istiab*, 2/581 (916) (Chosroes was a title given to Persian Kings)

an amazing divination. The Prophet's divination suggested that one of the two main powers of the era would be pushed into submission, and Suraka would possess the symbolic bracelets worn by its king. Suraka could not bring himself to believe such a thing, as he asked: "Are you talking about Chosroes, the son of Hurmuz?" The noble Messenger said: "Yes."

At the same time, this was a target given to Suraka and to all those who followed the Prophet. Suraka, a man who had left Mecca with the intention of killing the Prophet, was now returning as a Muslim with a sacred mission.

Many years after the incident, the Prophet's divination would become a reality during the Caliphate of Umar Ibn al-Khattab. Persia would be conquered by Umar who then would strip Chosroes off his bracelets and hand them over to Suraka. On this historical day, Umar would make the following statement:

> "Oh Suraka! Raise your arms and say: 'Glory be to Almighty who has taken these off Chosroes, the son of Hurmuz, a man who claimed that he was the lord of people, and handed them over to Suraka of the son of Mudleej, a man who came from a clan in the Arab desert.'"[49]

The entire incident had another dimension which involved Abu Bakr's father, Abu Kuhafa. As the old man came home to find that his son was missing, he asked where he was. All indications suggested that Abu Bakr had

---

[49] *Sunanu't-Bayhaki*, 6/357(12812)

left Mecca. This was not a joking matter. He had left everything behind to begin a new life. Abu Bakr had walked away from Mecca, his trade business, his children, relatives, friends, and his aging parents. A soul that had not been introduced to faith could not have comprehended this. Once faith had entered a heart, it gave certain power to its possessor. Depending on the level of faith, the possessor could accomplish things that would be incomprehensible to those who did not have faith. If it was necessary, the people of faith would even give up their families and relatives.

Without doubt, when Abu Bakr gave his word regarding migration to the noble Messenger, he did not even think about his family. Many years later, as they prepared for the battle of Tabuk, he said that he was placing his family under the protection of God and His Messenger. Perhaps, he was repeating the words he once uttered when he left Mecca for the great migration.

On the other hand, Abu Kuhafa could not understand Abu Bakr's migration. He kept on asking to everyone he came across: "Did he really do this? How could he leave his family behind and just take off like that?"[50] Abu Bakr had left, indeed, and without even looking back. This was exactly the kind of munificence that transformed Abu Kuhafa's son, Abdullah Ibn Uthman, into Abu Bakr. Abu Kuhafa bombarded his granddaughter, Asma with questions about her father's wealth: "I swear by God, he took

---

[50] Ibn Hisham, *as-Siratu'n-Nabawiyya*, 3/15

all his wealth with him, didn't he?" Asma replied hesitantly: "No grandfather! He left a great amount of his possessions to us."

Abu Kuhafa was an old man who was about to lose his eyesight. Asma used this to her advantage and gathered some pebbles. She then covered the pebbles with a piece of cloth and asked Abu Kuhafa to feel them. Finally, the grandfather was convinced.[51] Many years later, Asma explained the story, emphasizing that Abu Bakr had left nothing to them. Therefore, in order to console her grandfather, she had resorted to this solution.[52]

---

[51] Hakim, *Mustadrak*, 3/6 (4267)
[52] Ahmed b. Hanbal, *Musnad*, 6/350 (27006)

INITIAL YEARS IN MEDINA

The holy migration had concluded in Medina. God's Messenger was welcomed into the house of Ayyub al Ansari and Abu Bakr moved in with Harija Ibn Zaid. Abu Bakr was a man who would never take anything for granted. Like the other members of the Ansar, Harija offered him half of his wealth, but Abu Bakr kindly refused. He had five thousand dirhams, which he wanted to use as capital. He was an expert businessman, so he wanted to put his talent to work. Once again, Abu Bakr commenced his trade business in Medina. By his actions, he was teaching a lesson to the others who were close to the Prophet.

Sometime after, he sent a message to his son Abdullah, asking him to bring the rest of the family to Medina. The change of weather had affected Abu Bakr's health in a negative way, and he became quite ill. He was bed-ridden with a high fever. Abu Bakr's family was already looking for an opportunity to migrate to Medina. Before long, Abdullah brought his mother, Ummu Ruman, sisters Asma and Aisha, and the Prophet's daughters Fatima and Ummu Kulthum to Medina. Abu Kuhafa preferred to remain in Mecca. Although he would be left all alone, he could not comprehend the reason behind this migration.

Leaving Mecca was a difficult choice to make, but the believers had no other alternative. On the day that the Prophet left Mecca, he looked back and said: "I swear by God! You are the most blessed region by the side of God. Without doubt, I would have never left you if I wasn't forced out!"[53]

It was difficult for the immigrants to adjust to the conditions in Medina. For this reason, many of them came down with illnesses. High fever was the common symptom. Aisha asked for the Prophet's permission to visit her father. Abu Bakr was in the same room with Amr Ibn Fuhayra and Bilal Habashi.

Aisha approached her father. Abu Bakr was in great pain. His fever had almost rendered him unconscious. Aisha asked: "My dear father! How do you feel?" It was obvious that Abu Bakr was in a world of his own when he replied: "People sleep in the comfort of their homes, but they do not realize that death is closer to man than their own shoelaces."[54]

Aisha was confused. She assumed that Abu Bakr was not in a condition to make sense. This time she tried to talk to Amr: "Oh Amr...How do you feel!" Amr's condition was no different than that of Abu Bakr's. He began to mumble about death and being away from his hometown. She realized that it was no use talking to Amr either. As a last resort, she tried to speak to Bilal. He

---

[53] Ahmed b. Hanbal, *Musnad*, 5/393 (18364)
[54] *Sahih Bukhari*, 2/667 (1790)

seemed to be feeling somewhat better than the others. At least, he could sit up. Perhaps, he was recovering from the illness. Bilal spoke with a soft voice:

> Will I ever get the chance again? A chance to spend the night in the valleys of Mecca, amongst the smell of Ithir and Jalil plants?
>
> Will I ever drink from the water of Majanna while I stare at the beauty of Mt. Shame and Tafeel?

There was no difference in the emotional states of the three men. It was obvious that they missed Mecca, and this illness had made things worse. As soon as Aisha returned home, she explained everything to the noble Prophet. The Prophet of compassion quickly raised his hands, praying that God brought them to love Medina as He has made them love Mecca, and that He blessed the scales and measurements of that city and protected it from malaria.[55]

The Prophet's prayers were answered, and the illness moved away from Medina to the region of Jufa. From that day on, Medina would become the cradle of civilization and a hometown to believers...

---

[55] *Sahih Bukhari*, 2/667 (1790)

FUNHAS AND ABU BAKR

Inviting people to Islam was an ongoing duty for all believers. Naturally, Abu Bakr continued to convey the message in Medina. He interacted with people frequently and shared the depth of the divine revelations with everyone he met.

Occasionally, Abu Bakr visited a man called Funhas. This person had vast knowledge of the previous scriptures. He was a scholar who told stories mentioned in Torah to children at the synagogue. Funhas tried to educate children so that they may become future scholars. If this man embraced Islam, he would influence many people who respected him into accepting the last Prophet of God. One day, Abu Bakr visited him and began to talk about the essentials of faith. He made an emphasis on the life after death and mentioned the consequences of concealing the truth. Following a lengthy period of discussion, Abu Bakr said:

> Shame on you Funhas! Have fear in God, come and embrace Islam. You know very well that Muhammad is the Messenger sent by God. This is also clearly indicated in the Bible and the Torah.

Funhas had no intention of conceding to Abu Bakr. He began to ridicule the most fundamental issue of faith, as he replied to Abu Bakr's invitation:

> Oh Abu Bakr, I swear by God that we do not need him! God needs us. His requests from us are more than what we ask from him. We are wealthier than him. If God was wealthier than us, he would not have requested loans from our wealth, as suggested by your master. He forbids usury for you, yet he permits it for us. If he was wealthier than us, he would not have permitted usury.

Abu Bakr was a sensitive man who could not handle such insult aimed at God. With a devious manipulation, this man was trying to present coal as if they were diamonds. Moreover, his language was so profane. Before he could complete his sentence, Abu Bakr slapped him across the neck. This was something he never expected. Then Abu Bakr shouted:

> Oh enemy of God! I swear by the Almighty God, Who holds my life in His hand, I would have removed your head right now if it weren't for the agreement we have between us.

This was quite uncharacteristic of Abu Bakr because he was a kind man with a fragile posture. However, his stern stance in situations where God and His Messenger were in question could not be imitated by even the bravest.

Funhas had been beaten up due to his unrestrained behavior. Quickly, he went to the Prophet to lodge a complaint about Abu Bakr. The evidence of harassment was quite visible. However, it seemed like he had not learned his lesson yet, as he tried to blame Abu Bakr for the entire incident. Funhas did not mention anything about the insults he had made. The noble Messenger quickly summoned Abu Bakr and asked why he did that. Abu Bakr displayed a sense of timidity, but he had to show the true face of this vile man. He was complaining to a man whom he had insulted. Under normal circumstances, Abu Bakr was not fond of defending his own actions. However, in this case, he had to tell it as it happened. Therefore, Abu Bakr explained:

> Oh noble Messenger of God! This man is an enemy of God. He has committed a great sin. He said terrible things about the Almighty God. He claimed that God is poor and that they are wealthier than God. I could not control my temper, and I hit him for God's sake.

Funhas became panicky upon hearing the matter as it had happened. His only solution was to deny Abu Bakr's claim. "I did not say any of these! he replied." What kind of a man was this? He was accusing Abu Bakr of lying. Perhaps, once the barriers of truth were breached, there was no turning back.

Before long, divine verses that confirmed Abu Bakr's faithfulness were revealed. The heavens above began to speak, and the Archangel Gabriel brought down the Qur'anic revelation to Prophet Muhammad, peace and blessings be upon him. The verses mentioned the words spoken by Funhas and explained that such people of hypocrisy and two-facedness would be punished in hellfire.[56]

---

[56] Ibn Hisham, *as-Siratu'n-Nabawiyya*, 3/96-97

TOWARDS THE BATTLE OF BADR

Their hearts were at the Ka'ba and in Mecca... People like Utba, Uqba, Shayba, Abu Lahab, and Abu Jahl were back in Mecca... Believers, with their divine guide, the noble Prophet were living a peaceful life in Medina. The serenity of being able to fulfill their obligations towards God was inimitable. However, the filthy hands of the non-believers would not let them be even in Medina. Their feelings of resentment increased with each passing day as they blamed themselves for letting the believers slip away from their hands.

Finally, their paths crossed at Badr. This was the first time they would meet on the battle field. Extreme measures needed to be taken because years of work depended on it. This was the day of reckoning where the hearts that beat for God would face an army three times larger than theirs. For this reason, the noble Messenger of God opened his arms and raised his hands, beseeching the help of his Lord: "Oh Lord! If this community is defeated here, on this day, there will be no one left to serve you! Grant us victory, oh Lord!"

As the noble Messenger continued to pray, Abu Bakr picked up his garment, which had fallen off his shoulders, and placed it back on the Prophet's shoulders. Then he supported the Prophet's prayer with the following words: "Do not worry, oh noble Messenger of God! Glad tidings to you, for God shall grant the promised victory you request!"

There was no doubt in the mind of the Prophet. A few minutes ago he had pointed to the exact spots and informed them where certain non-believers would lose their lives. Then he had made the following statement: "God has promised victory!"[57]

This meant that each believer had to fulfill his duty. Abu Bakr knew exactly what he had to do and that was to provide spiritual support. Following the prayer, the noble Messenger was resting in the tent when he suddenly jumped up and faced Abu Bakr. Then he made the following historical statement: "Glad tidings to you, oh Abu Bakr! Without doubt, God's help to you has arrived. Here is Gabriel waiting for orders, as he rides his heavily breathing horse."[58]

All the preparations had been made, and it was time to draw the swords. The noble Messenger walked out of his tent and made a gesture of encouragement to his army. Finally, the battle had begun. Before long, the promised victory was granted. The Quraysh, who had come to Badr to solve the issue once and for all, returned to Mecca with slogans of revenge. They had suffered a significant defeat. Besides the amount of men they had

---

[57] *Sahih Ibn Hebban*, 11/114 (4793) 431
[58] Abu Ja'far et-Tabari, *er-Riyadu'n-Nadera*, 2/35

lost on the battle field, they were leaving behind seventy of their soldiers who were captured by the believers.

The noble Messenger chose the middle path with every decision he had made. Following the battle, he explained to his Companions, how the prisoners should be treated. Some of the Companions, such as Umar argued that they should all be killed. However, Abu Bakr suggested they should be released for a certain amount of ransom. He argued that the income would be used for strengthening the military. The noble Prophet was thinking along the same lines. He accepted Abu Bakr's proposal. According to this agreement, literate prisoners would be released on the condition that they taught ten Muslims how to read and write. Those who were illiterate would be released if they paid certain amount of ransom.[59]

As fate would have it, Abu Bakr's oldest son Abdurrahman was in the lines of the Qurayshi army. He was prepared to fight against his own father.

As the battle began, Abu Bakr wanted to confront his son and engage in combat, but the Prophet did not give him permission. Perhaps, the noble Messenger knew that one day Abdurrahman would come and submit to the truth. For this reason, the Prophet did not wish to give Abdurrahman an excuse to refrain from the truth.

---

[59] Abu Nuaym, *Hilyetu'l-Awliya*, 1/43

Many years later, when Abdurrahman finally came to submit[60], they had a conversation about the incident at Badr. As Abdurrahman described his emotional state, he said that if his father Abu Bakr had confronted him on that day, he would not have drawn his sword against him. Abu Bakr, on the other hand, had other ideas. He declared that for the sake of God he would have fought his son and killed him, if it was inevitable.[61]

---

[60] Abdurrahman was also in the army of the non-believers at Uhud. He embraced Islam later, during the incident at Hudaybiya.

[61] Halebi, *Siratu'l-Halebiyya*, 2/374

THE MAN OF THE BATTLE FIELDS

Abu Bakr had proven himself at Badr and continued to display an unrivaled courage by standing next to the Prophet in all the battles that followed. He was a man of great self-sacrifice. On the day of Uhud, he was one of the few who stayed by the Prophet at a stage when things had gotten out of control. When the noble Messenger saw Abu Bakr draw his sword and charge towards the enemy lines, all alone, he said: "Put your sword back, oh Abu Bakr! Do not make us sad by sacrificing yourself!"[62]

Abu Bakr had his mind on the job ahead, so much so that he could not even hear the Prophet's call. The Prophet had to repeat himself. Finally, Abu Bakr heard the noble voice of the Messenger. Quickly, he turned back from the martyrdom, for which he had been longing.

On the day of Tabuk, the Messenger of God had handed the banner of Islam to Abu Bakr. It was a large black banner that Abu Bakr had to carry against the armies of Byzantium. He was a man of balance. This unique quality of Abu Bakr always prevailed during incidents such as Badr, Uhud, Handaq, and Hudaybiya. He was always

---

[62] Abu Ja'far et-Tabari, *er-Riyadu'n-Nadera*, 2/46

there to help the Prophet establish harmony amongst the Companions. The effort he displayed during all the battles was beyond comprehension. At every battle, his main duty was to protect the Prophet and for this cause he would have given his life without the slightest of hesitations.

Even in situations where emotions were at an extreme level, he would not deviate from the straight path. He lived and breathed righteousness. It was Abu Bakr who consoled and convinced Umar during the days of confusion at Hudaybiya. Although, the contents of the agreement appeared to be negative from the believers' perspective, in reality, Hudaybiya was a great victory.

On that significant day, Abu Bakr held Umar by the hand and in a stern manner, he said: "Without doubt, he is the Messenger of God! He would not rebel against God! He has the support of the Almighty! Do not desert him and never disobey him! I swear by God, he is on the true path!"[63]

Abu Bakr had never left the side of his beloved master. He was also the greatest supporter of the Prophet on critical days such as Tabuk and Hunayn. Umar Ibn al-Khattab explains an incident that occurred on the day of Tabuk:

> We were on our way to Tabuk at a time when tensions were quite high. Following a long grueling journey, we stopped at a certain location to rest. We were severely dehydrated. There were people amongst us who had slaughtered their camels to use the liquid

---

[63] *Sahih Muslim*, 3/1411 (1785)

inside the animal to cool themselves down. Upon seeing this, Abu Bakr came to the Prophet and said:

"Oh Messenger of God! Without doubt, God answers your prayers with a blessing. Would you pray for us?"

Were there any other options other than resorting to the Creator of causes at a time when physical causes had failed? The Prophet asked: "Do you really wish for this?" The reply came quickly, and it was from the heart: "Yes!"

The noble Messenger raised his hands at once and began to beseech help from God. He had not even completed his prayer yet when strong winds began to blow. A short while later, clouds appeared above us and brought the much needed cool weather.

The Muslim army cooled down with the winds brought by this sanctified prayer. As the men prepared to march, they came face to face with another miracle. It was raining, but only on the area that the army had camped. The landscape surrounding the campsite remained sunny and dry.

ABU BAKR'S PLACE BY THE PROPHET'S SIDE

The rank of those who supported the cause even at times of extreme adversity had to be special. These individuals had a unique place by the side of God. The Almighty God explains this distinction in the following verse:

> Not equal among you are those who spend before the victory comes and fight (for God's sake, and those who do not): they are greater in rank than those who spend after the victory comes and fight later. However, to all God has promised what is the best (paradise). God is fully aware of all that you do.[64]

Without question, the Prophet's manner was no different. Those who stood by his side in the early days had a unique value. Indeed, no one could have imagined the enormity of the rewards earned by those who stood by the Prophet's side at times when predicaments rained upon them. The noble Messenger was an inimitable mirror that reflected God's etiquette. How could he have treated these people any other way?

---

[64] Hadid 57:10

Abu Bakr's Place by the Prophet's Side

The divine cause that began with the reunion at Mt. Hira had found exceptional support right from the beginning. Those who had supported him from the word go, particularly those who were the first of the firsts, had a different place in the Prophet's heart. And the Prophet made this quite clear at every opportunity and reflected it in his attitude towards them.

One day, God's Messenger was sitting with his Companions when he saw his beloved friend approach. He seemed emotionally distressed. At first, the noble Messenger analyzed his appearance from a distance. Then he said: "Something has happened to our friend!"

He knew his friend very well. Abu Bakr's face had gone pale, and his body showed signs of intense exhaustion. He came and sat next to the Prophet. Then timidly he began to explain:

> Something happened between Umar Ibn al-Khattab and me. I think I acted a bit hastily and broke his heart. I felt regret instantly and apologized to him, but he did not accept it. So, I came to you, oh noble Messenger of God.

The Prophet was saddened by Abu Bakr's despondency. He could not stand to see his loyal friend in such condition. At first, he made a prayer: "May God have mercy on Abu Bakr!"

This was the nature of the Prophet. He became joyful with the joy of his loved ones and sad with their sadness.

Suddenly, the atmosphere changed, it was as if dark clouds had appeared above them.

Meanwhile, Umar had also regretted his own behavior and went to Abu Bakr's house to apologize. He could not find Abu Bakr at home, so Umar rushed towards the mosque. His emotional state was no different to that of Abu Bakr's. He greeted the Prophet and walked into the Masjid. Umar could sense the tension as he found a place to sit. He was feeling great regret, but it was too late. He could not rewind the clock and undo what he had done. At that instant, the great Umar seemed as if all the energy had been drained out of him. Abu Bakr's heart could not take it anymore. He threw himself at the feet of the noble Prophet and implored: "By God! I caused wrongdoing! It was my fault!"

He was so sincere that he kept on repeating the same words with a tone of voice that begged for forgiveness. The clouds that were loaded with rain was about to burst with mercy. The noble Messenger targeted the entire congregation as he said:

> I swear by God! When God sent me as a Messenger, all of you claimed that I was lying! Abu Bakr was the only one who said, "You speak the truth!" He protected me with his life and possessions! Should you not leave my (loyal) supporter to me?[65]

What could you say to such truthful words? The heads were bowed in affirmation. Like a silent chorus, everyone

---

[65] *Sahih Bukhari*, 4/1701 (4364)

was singing the same tune: "You spoke the truth, o noble Messenger." Even in situations where his heart was broken, Abu Bakr thought about the feelings of others. He thought about the sorrow that the other person felt and blamed himself for being the cause. As Abu Bakr walked away from the gathering, he wept silently.

This was his character. He could not have behaved any other way. Unfortunately, from time to time, these things occurred. On another occasion, he had a misunderstanding with Rabiat'ul Aslami. The issue was brought before the Prophet. Abu Bakr had uttered a word that hurt Rabia's feelings. He tried to make up as he asked Rabia to say the same things back to him. Unfortunately, Rabia refused and Abu Bakr said: "Either you take what is rightfully yours or I will take this matter to the noble Prophet."

Rabia's attitude did not change. It was obvious that the only way they could solve the issue was to ask for the Prophet's help. Swiftly, they came to him. At that point, a group of men from the Aslam clan were sitting with the Prophet. They had already heard about the incident. They were criticizing Abu Bakr's behavior, when Rabia intervened:

> Be quite! You are talking about Abu Bakr here, not just any person! God refers to him as "the second one of the two" in the cave of Thawr. Do not speak against him, in my defense! The Prophet will be saddened by his sadness. Without doubt, the Prophet's sorrow will bring the wrath of God upon us! And that would mean the end of Rabia!

Abu Bakr explained everything that had occurred. The Prophet's expression suggested that he was not pleased with what he had heard. He looked at Rabia and asked with an unpleased tone of voice about his problem with Abu Bakr. Rabia was also saddened by the whole affair. However, he wished to clarify the issue. There was a small detail which they had overlooked. Rabia said: "Oh noble Messenger, he said some unpleasant words to me. Then he suggested that I say the same thing back at him. However, I declined." God's Messenger was pleased with Rabia's behavior. He advised Rabia to say: "May God embrace you with His mercy, oh Abu Bakr!"

Clearly, the Prophet did not wish to disconcert his beloved friend who has been by his side since the beginning. For this reason, he was asking Rabia to say a prayer for him. The Prophet's support for him, even in a situation where he may have been in the wrong, touched Abu Bakr's heart so deeply that he began to weep. According to Rabia's testimony, Abu Bakr burst into tears as he sat in the corner.[66]

---

[66] Hakim, *Mustadrak*, 2/189 (2718)

HIS MATURITY AND ABILITY TO COMPREHEND

He was one of the most erudite individuals amongst the believers, yet he never used this as an advantage to build a reputation. He had witnessed almost all of the revelations that came down to the Prophet and possessed knowledge about the most honorable Prophetic traditions. Perhaps, this is why he was one of the two people who gave a *fatwa* (ruling) while the Prophet was still alive.

However, he had concealed his wisdom so much so that he would not speak unless he was approached with a question. He preferred to let others ask questions to the Prophet so that everyone obtained information about the matter at hand. People like Abu Bakr were so sensitive that when they sat next to the Prophet, they behaved as if there were birds on their heads. They trembled at the prospect of disturbing the Prophet. In reference to this, he had once made the following statement: "What realm would accept me or under which sky would I find refuge, if I make a remark that contradicts God's book."[67]

One day, the following verses were revealed: *Not your desires, nor those of the People of the Book (can prevail): whoev-*

---
[67] Ibn Ebi Shayba, *Musannaf*, 6/136 (30103)

er works evil, will be requited accordingly. Nor will he find, besides God, any protector or helper.[68]

Abu Bakr went into deep contemplation upon hearing the verse. He was pondering the contents of the divine verse. It seemed as if there was no way out for Abu Bakr. How could the son of Abu Kuhafa sleep on such a night? Quickly, he went to the Prophet of God. His face had turned white, and his heart was beating like a drum. With a trembling voice, he asked: "O noble Messenger! This verse has broken our backs. Is there anyone amongst us who does not make a mistake?"

Once again, it was up to the noble Prophet to console Abu Bakr. He looked deep into his eyes and reminded Abu Bakr of daily strife and toils that people have to go through. Then the Prophet concluded: "These are the things for which you will be rewarded in the afterlife."[69]

On another occasion when Abu Bakr was sitting with the Prophet, a man came and began to curse him. Being next to the Prophet, he felt extremely mortified. He could not give any meaning to the behavior of this outrageous man. He took a glance with the corner of his eye to see the Prophet's reaction. The noble Messenger was smiling and this produced a trifling comfort in Abu Bakr's heart.

Unfortunately, the man had no intention of quitting as he continued with his insults and abuse. Finally, Abu Bakr could not take it anymore. He decided to intervene with a reply. Before he could say a few words in his defense, the noble Mes-

---

[68] Nisa 4/123
[69] *Sahih Ibn Hebban*, 7/170 (2910)

senger stood up and left the scene. The noble Messenger was not smiling anymore. Upon seeing this, Abu Bakr also stood up and swiftly rushed after the Prophet. He could not bear to see the Prophet upset. When he caught up with the Prophet, he said: "Oh noble Messenger of God!" Then in a most respectful manner, he asked: "You were there when that man was insulting me. I tried to stop him when he transgressed his limits. Why did you leave the gathering with anger?"

Abu Bakr behaved modestly as he attempted to comprehend the lesson that the noble Prophet was teaching with his body language. The Prophet paused for a brief moment and then made a statement that should be memorized by all Muslims:

> Without doubt, as you remained silent, an angel was there to reply on your behalf. As soon as you began to defend yourself, Satan appeared. I did not wish to be in the same place with Satan.

Following his explanation, the noble Prophet generalized the issue with additional comments:

> Oh Abu Bakr! Three things are true:
> God will exalt and reward those who keep their silence for the sake of God when they undergo wrongdoing.
> Whoever opens a door in the name of good and gives generously to those close to him, God will increase his wealth and grant prosperity.
> Whoever asks from others for the sake of more wealth, God will increase his poverty.[70]

---

[70] Ahmed b. Hanbal, *Musnad*, 2/436 (9622)

THE INITIAL SIGNS OF DEPARTURE

Just as his depth in wisdom, his sagacity and discernment were at an unreachable height. From the first words uttered, he would comprehend the sentence and understood where it was leading. As the day of departure approached, the noble Messenger delivered a sermon. In one section of the sermon, he said: "God granted his servant a choice between this world and that which is with Him, and the servant has chosen the latter."

Perhaps, no one understood what the Prophet was signifying. However, Abu Bakr covered his face with both hands as he wept loudly in the corner. Those who saw Abu Bakr could not comprehend why he had reacted so severely to a statement like that. In confusion, they were asking why he had begun to weep. According to Abu Bakr, the person who was given a choice was no other than the Prophet himself. The statement suggested that the time of separation was near. The thought of the Prophet's departure after many years together had touched an extremely delicate spot in Abu Bakr's heart. He could not stop weeping.

Once again, the noble Messenger who had to console Abu Bakr. The Prophet knew that Abu Bakr had understood the meaning of his statement. He said: "Do not weep, oh Abu Bakr...do not weep." Then, with a higher tone of voice, the Prophet said that when wealth and friendship is in concern, Abu Bakr was the most reliable of all human beings, and that if he were to attain a true friend, he would have declared Abu Bakr as the "Khalil" (the genuine friend). However, from this point on, there is brotherhood and love in Islam. Close all doors which open to the Masjid, but leave Abu Bakr's door opened.[71]

Abu Bakr's value next to the Prophet was so immense that even when the Prophet hinted his own departure from this world, he consoled Abu Bakr who was saddened by the news. In addition, the Prophet praised and complimented him by declaring that all doors should be closed, except for Abu Bakr's door. It was obvious that the spiritual atmosphere in Abu Bakr's home was no different to the one in the mosque.

---

[71] *Sahih Bukhari*, 1/77 (454)

A MAN OF TRUST AND RELIABILITY

Regardless of his deep knowledge in Islam, he relied totally on the Messenger of God. When a certain issue was in concern, the views of the Prophet were enough for him. If there was a saying of the Prophet regarding the matter at hand, the perspective of others did not matter anymore. According to Abu Bakr, the noble Messenger always had the last word.

In those days, there were two superpowers in the region, the Byzantine Empire and the Persian Empire. A great battle had erupted between the two powers, and the Persians, who worshipped fire, had attained victory over the Byzantine army, who were considered as the People of the Book. Byzantium had been hit so severely that no one believed the Byzantines could ever stand on their feet again.

What significance could such victory have on the region of Hejaz? Indeed, it had vital consequences because the idol worshippers of Mecca, who derived meanings from every occurrence and event, used such information to oppress the Muslims. The great battle also carried another importance; it was a battle between belief in one God and polytheism. The victory of the fire-worshippers over the Christians was used by the Quraysh to argue that they would do the same thing to Muslims. The Quraysh was on the side of the Persians. This was an opportunity for them because an earthly power had prevailed over the heavenly power. According to their logic, an earthly power such as the Quraysh would also attain victory over the Muslims, who were regarded as heavenly.

During the course of the debate, Surah Rum was revealed, and the Qur'an stated that within three to nine years, the Byzantine Empire would defeat the Persians. This was great news for the Quraysh who decided to use it as a material to ridicule the Muslims. According to them, the Qur'an predicted the impossible. When Ubayy Ibn Halaf ran into Abu Bakr, he brought up the subject. He began to talk about this verse and tried to make mockery of it. Abu Bakr had no doubts about the prediction and defended the Qur'an vigorously. Both of them were relentless in their arguments, so they decided to place a stake on it. According to the agreement, in the conclusion of the third year, the loser would give ten camels to the winner.

Abu Bakr then went to the Prophet quickly and informed him of their agreement. The noble Prophet reminded Abu Bakr about the period signified by the verse. The verse clearly indicated that the incident would take within three to nine years. However, Abu Bakr had interpreted it as three years. The Prophet suggested that Abu Bakr amend the agreement by increasing the years and the amount of camels placed as stakes.

Upon receiving the Prophet's advice, Abu Bakr went back to Ubayy Ibn Halaf and proposed that the period be increased to nine years and the number of camels placed as stakes also increased. According to Ubayy, this made no difference because no one in the Arabian Peninsula believed that the Persians could ever be defeated. The deal was done.

Nine long years had passed and in the year 627, the two armies had met once again. In the great battle of Ninova, the miraculous verses of the Qur'an prevailed. The Byzantine army defeated the great Persian Empire. Around the same time, Muslims confronted the idol-worshippers at Badr, where again the victory promised by God was attained. Muslims experienced great joy as they had defeated God's enemies, whom they met in combat for the first time. They praised and glorified God. The Quraysh sustained a second blow with the news of the Byzantine victory over the Persians. Things had not developed according to their expectations. Moreover, they had also suffered annihilation at Badr. Contrary to their speculations, the Qur'an had triumphed.[72]

Ubayy had already gone to the place where he belonged. For this reason, Abu Bakr went to his heirs and requested one hundred camels. Their traditions compelled them to abide by the agreement, and they handed one hundred camels over to Abu Bakr. What would a benevolent man like Abu Bakr do with these camels? Obviously, give them to charity. Abu Bakr did what was necessary and donated the camels to the needy.[73]

---

[72] The verse clearly states that Muslims would also rejoice on the same day. Qur'an, Surah Rum: 30/2-5

[73] *Tafsiru Ibn Kesr*, 3/405

MODESTY AND SINCERITY

One day, the noble Prophet was delivering a sermon when he paused and asked: "Is there anyone amongst you observing the fast today?" Following a short period of silence, Abu Bakr replied timidly that he was fasting. God's Messenger, asked again: "Did anyone give to charity?" Once again, there was total silence, followed by the timid voice of Abu Bakr: "I gave, oh noble Messenger." The questions continued: "Has anyone gone to a funeral prayer?" It was as if the noble Messenger was having a conversation with one person only. Abu Bakr replied again: "I did." The Prophet continued to ask: "Have any of you fed a starving person today?" There was no change in the process. It was obvious that the noble Messenger was presenting his dear friend as an exemplary figure to his people. He knew that Abu Bakr would never mention these virtues if it left were up to him. Once Again, Abu Bakr replied to the Prophet's question: "I did, oh noble Messenger." It was time for the noble Prophet to make the final statement. He held everyone as witnesses to his testimony as he explained: "Whoever performs these deeds in a day, will be forgiven of his sins and paradise will be due for him."[74]

---

[74] *Sahih Muslim*, 2/713 (1028)

THE PHILANTHROPIST

Abu Bakr led the pack of devotees who had placed their lives and wealth on the line for the divine cause. As he sacrificed everything for God, he never stopped to think for a minute about the future. He gave fearlessly. As he distributed his wealth, God replaced it with more as a token of Abu Bakr's gratitude. Personally, he lived as if he was the poorest man in the region of Hejaz while he brought everything he possessed to the Prophet so that it may be used for the cause.

One day, the noble Messenger was speaking to the people when someone mentioned the early days and how Muslims suffered so much torment. In those days, Abu Bakr was considered one of the wealthiest persons in Mecca. He had accumulated riches to the value of forty thousand dirhams. As soon as he had embraced Islam, he began to distribute his wealth in the name of God. He had given so much that when he came to Medina he had five thousand dirhams left over. The noble Prophet described Abu Bakr's philanthropy with the following statement: "I have not benefitted from anyone's wealth as much as I did from Abu Bakr's."

A man like Abu Bakr preferred to conceal his virtues at all times. He felt so mortified that he went to the corner of the Masjid and began to weep as if he had committed a sin. Without doubt, he had given his word from the beginning to sacrifice all he had for the sake of God. A few minutes later, he regained his composure and replied timidly: "May my wealth and myself be sacrificed on your path, oh noble Messenger of God! Everything I have is yours!"[75]

At times of desperation when others gave immensely and believed that they had surpassed Abu Bakr, he came and gave everything he had. No one could outshine Abu Bakr when it came to giving in the name of God. He had no concerns about the future. His trust and submission to God and His Messenger was so powerful that he had placed even his family, the people he was responsible of, under the protection of God and His Messenger. His sincerity and Loyalty was crystal clear.

On many occasions, he suffered the pains of starvation, yet he told no one. You could not even hear a tiny complaint from him. Sometimes he would hit the streets looking for something to eat, and quite often, he would run into the Prophet. He would then become concerned with the Prophet's condition and forgot about his own burdens.

One day, the Prophet was having a conversation with his Ashab. Abu Bakr was sitting in the corner listening to the divine words flowing from the Prophet's mouth. He was wearing an old garment, the collar of which was attached by a thorn. Abu Bakr, the prominent wealthy businessman of Mecca, was now living in poverty. He

---

[75] Halebi, *es-Siratu'l-Halebiyya*, 2/200

could not even find proper clothes to wear. However, he was not in this situation due to a lack of means. He had sacrificed everything he had so that others did not suffer. This was a quality that had a special place by the side of God. Suddenly, the Angel Gabriel appeared. He greeted the Prophet and then turned towards Abu Bakr. The angel asked: "Oh Abu Bakr! What is this garment you wear? Why did you attach its collar with a thorn?"

Certainly, the angel knew the answer, but he would pass judgment depending on the reply. The Messenger of God replied: "Oh Gabriel! This man distributed all of his wealth for my cause prior to the conquering of Mecca!"

The angel had found the right moment to share the glad tidings: "Tell Abu Bakr that God sends him His greetings! God has a question for him, "As a poor man, is Abu Bakr happy with his Lord?"

What could Abu Bakr do in such situation where his unique virtues were confirmed by the angel? He burst into tears as he wept loudly. Abu Bakr had received a greeting from the Almighty, and He was asking if Abu Bakr was happy. He had to reply. He spoke with great difficulty: "How could I be unhappy with my Lord? How could I turn away from Him? I am pleased with you, oh Lord…I am pleased with you, oh Lord!"[76]

Perhaps this is why Abu Bakr and Umar were the grand viziers of the Prophet on earth, just as Gabriel and Mikhail were in the heavens.

---

[76] Isbahani, *Hilyetu'l-Awliya*, 7/105

There was not a day in which Abu Bakr did not visit the Prophet. Being so close to his sanctified presence made Abu Bakr a fortunate target for Prophetic compliments. On a day when they stood on Mt. Uhud, the mountain was shaken by an earthquake, and the Prophet shouted, "Calm down oh mountain, for there is a Prophet, a Siddiq, and martyrs standing on top of you!" This was information regarding the future, and it had come from the heavens and beyond.

The noble Prophet, who had given glad tidings of paradise to Abu Bakr on many occasions, once said: "Oh People! You should know that Abu Bakr has never done an act to displease me!"[77] With this statement, the Prophet showed the importance of the link that existed between obedience and Loyalty. Generally, the ten individuals who were given the guarantee of paradise had a special place by the side of the Prophet. This was quite evident in their social lives. These individuals represented the firsts. During the battles, they would take their place in front of the Prophet, and during the daily prayers they would line up right behind the Prophet. This was quite customary, and others accepted it.

Amongst all men, Abu Bakr was the Prophet's favorite. He loved him more than anyone else. He was his grand vizier. Sometimes he would use him as a clerk of the divine revelations and when it was necessary, he would guide him in teaching others how to behave next to the

---

[77] Abu Ja'far et-Tabari, *er-Riyadu'n-Nadera*, 1/227

Prophet when they visited him. For this reason, the noble Prophet once said: "Just as you were my friend in the cave, you will also be a master standing over my pond (in paradise)."[78] The noble Prophet, peace and blessings be upon him, complimented Abu Bakr on many occasions.

Abu Bakr never expected anything in return for the good he did for people. He only wished for the reward of God. He never reminded people of the help he provided for them. He refrained from hurting their feelings and breaking honor. The noble Prophet was aware of this quality and always commended him for this.

He had wed his daughter Aisha to the Messenger of God. Aisha was the mother of all believers. Although she was his daughter, Abu Bakr valued and respected her like a mother. Following the Qur'anic revelation, Aisha was no longer Abu Bakr's daughter, but she was the mother of all believers.

When Hypocrite slanderers had accused Aisha of immorality, Mistah Ibn Usasah was amongst those who were taken in by the rumors even though he was a man who lived in poverty, and Abu Bakr was the only person who supported him.

Abu Bakr felt great sorrow in his heart when he heard that Mistah was amongst those who believed the rumors about his daughter. Because of the delicate sensitivity he had towards religion, Abu Bakr ceased his financial support to Mistah. Before long the following verses were revealed:

---

[78] *Sunanu't-Tirmidhi*, 5/613 (3670)

> Let not those among you who are favored with resources swear that they will no longer give to the kindred, the needy, and those who have emigrated in God's cause. Rather, let them pardon and forbear. Do you not wish that God should forgive you? God is All-Forgiving, All-Compassionate. [79]

Abu Bakr was a man who lived his life according to the divine revelations. He repented at once and said: "I swear by God that I wish to be forgiven by Him!"

Then, he continued his financial support of Mistah. He had made a promise to himself: "By God! I will continue to provide this help without any delay!"[80] Perhaps, this was the reason why all the gates of paradise were open to Abu Bakr.

One day, the noble Messenger explained that for every good deed performed by an individual, there is a different gate that opens to paradise. Abu Bakr was curious as he asked: "Is there a person who could be summoned to all the gates of paradise?" The noble Messenger replied: "Yes, and I anticipate that you will be one of them!"[81]

Abu Bakr, may God be pleased with him, was one of the unique individuals who interpreted dreams in the presence of the noble Prophet.

---

[79] Qur'an, Nur 24:22
[80] *Sahih Muslim*, 4/2136 (432)
[81] *Sunanu'n-Nesai*, 5/9 (2439)

In reference to his distinctive place by the side of the Prophet, Said Ibn Musayyab, one of the fortunate ones who met the Companions of the Prophet, stated:

> Abu Bakr was like a grand vizier to the Prophet, peace and blessings be upon him. He would consult him on all issues. He was the second person in Islam, the second person in the cave, the second person in the booth on the day of Badr, and the second person in the grave. The noble Messenger of God did not place anyone before him.[82]

---

[82] Hakim, *Mustadrak*, 3/66 (4408)

THE DAY OF THE CONQUEST

The polytheists had broken the conditions of the truce signed at Hudaybiya by ambushing a village in the middle of the night and spilling blood. This was a clear sign; thus, a Surah revealed on the day of Hudaybiya gave the joyful tidings of victory over Mecca. The revelations informed Muslims that the conquest would soon take place.[83] This meant that the time had arrived. God's Messenger asked Aisha to prepare rations for the journey. However, it had to be kept as a secret.

As Aisha prepared for the journey, her father Abu Bakr came by the house. He was an intelligent man who quickly realized that something was going on. He began to ask one question after another. However, Aisha, the mother of believers chose to remain silent. Abu Bakr could not get a word out of Aisha. A leading figure like Abu Bakr could not be kept in the dark about significant developments. Hastily, he went to the noble Prophet. He began to ask the same questions to the noble Prophet. This time, there was an answer for all of them:

"Are we preparing for a military expedition, oh noble Messenger of God?"

---

[83] *Qur'an*, Surah Fetih: 48/27

"Yes!" replied the Prophet.

"The sons of Asfar?"

"No!"

"The people of Najeed?"

"No!"

"Then it must be the Quraysh?"

"Yes!"

"All right, oh noble Messenger of God. But don't we have a treaty with them?"

"Yes we had…you must not have heard what they did in the region of the sons of Ka'b."

Abu Bakr realized that the big day had come. Quickly, he also began to prepare for the journey.

Finally, a force of ten thousand men left Medina. As they approached Mecca, they camped on a high point. God's Messenger ordered each man to light a fire. Seeing the thousands of bonfires burning nearby, the Quraysh was caught unprepared. Soon, they began to panic realizing that they did not possess the power to fight against such a large army. The amount of bonfires suggested that there were at least fifty thousand men approaching Mecca. The reason for this was that in those days, traditionally, people would gather into small groups of five to six persons, and each group would light a bonfire. According to this logic, the number of men in the approaching army could have been a hundred thousand.

Abu Sufyan, the chieftain of Mecca at the time, realized that combat was out of the question because of the imbalance between the two forces. Therefore, he decided to solve the matter with an agreement. He came to the campsite to talk with people he knew personally. He wanted to convince them to withdraw from Mecca. Abu Bakr was amongst the people he visited. He approached Abu Bakr and insisted that on rewriting the agreement and increasing the period of the treaty. However, Abu Bakr was not a man who would make a decision on such a strategic matter. Thinking about the Prophet, he said: "My perspective is no different to that of the noble Messenger of God." Then he added: "I swear by God! If I heard that grains and seeds had declared war against you, I would support them."[84]

This was an example of shrewdness, and it was said to the face of the enemy in an undeterred manner. There was nothing else that Abu Sufyan could do. So he returned to Mecca empty handed. Finally, Mecca was conquered and the refugees, who were once expelled from their beloved land, returned to their homes.

Abu Bakr had an important duty that could not wait. Swiftly, he rushed to the house of his aging father. With a beseeching manner, he tried to address the old man's soul. Islam had prevailed, and the time for Abu Kuhafa had come. Nothing could make Abu Bakr happier. He held Abu Kuhafa by the hand and took him to the Prophet, peace and blessings be upon him.

When the Messenger of God saw the father and son approach, he stood up and said: "Oh Abu Bakr! Why did

---

[84] Salaba, *el-Inshirahu wa Rafu'd-diki bi Sirate Abu Bakr as-Siddiq*, 96

you bring him all the way to us? We could have gone to him."

This also meant that it was time to conquer the hearts and souls of the people. Did not the old man who stood at an intersection deserve such compliment? Abu Bakr also became emotional upon such a flattering remark. He thought about the situation that the noble Messenger was in and the conditions surrounding the conquering of Mecca. Then, he replied: "It was more appropriate for him to come before your presence, oh Messenger of God."

Tears of joy began to flow with the testimony of Abu Kuhafa: "I bear witness that there is no god but God! And I bear witness that Muhammad is God's Messenger!" The Prophet was so joyous that he also congratulated Abu Bakr for his father's decision. Abu Kuhafa was an obedient servant who now recognized his God. Moreover, this servant was the father of the Prophet's closest friend. For this reason, the noble Prophet advised Abu Bakr to spend more time with his father and suggested that he should dye his hair and change its style.[85]

Abu Bakr was the happiest person on earth since his father had also embraced Islam. Another important thing about Abu Bakr was the fact that he was the only person whose entire family had become Companions. His father, mother, children, and grandchildren were all Muslims.

---

[85] Taberane, *al-Mu'jamu'l-Kabir*, 24/88 (236)

THE LEADER OF PILGRIMS

It was the eighth year of the great migration. Hajj had become an obligatory act of worship. The noble Prophet did not participate in the initial Hajj. He assigned Abu Bakr as the leader of the first Hajj. They left Medina with a group of three hundred pilgrims. This was a Hajj duty that would be performed for the first time.

Following their departure, new Qur'anic revelations came down. In order to inform them, the noble Prophet sent Ali after them. According to the latest revelations, polytheists and atheists were not permitted to enter the Ka'ba anymore. Also, this sacred building that was built in the name of God would not be circled by naked people anymore. The Ka'ba was the first place of worship that was built in the name of God.

THE FAREWELL PILGRIMAGE

In the second year, after the Major Pilgrimage became an obligatory duty, the Prophet led his people. This was the first Pilgrimage for the Prophet, but it was obvious that it would also be his last. As the Prophet spoke to his people at Arafat, his statements suggested that this was a farewell sermon: "Without doubt, God has given a choice to his servant. This was a choice between what He has prepared for him by His side and this world."

As he continued to speak, he would pause in certain intervals to ask: "Have I performed my duty?" When the loud reply of thousands echoed through Arafat, acknowledging that the Prophet had performed his duty, he shouted as he raised his finger and pointed to the heavens: "Oh Lord! Be my witness!"

Then God Almighty revealed the verse that finalized Arafat: "This day I have perfected for you your Religion."[86] This scene touched a deep spot in the hearts of those sensitive individuals, such as Abu Bakr. At first, he said: "May our fathers and mothers be sacrificed to you, oh Messenger of God!"

---
[86] *Qur'an*, Maida 5:3

He was feeling an indescribable sorrow in his soul. He knew that it was the Messenger of God who was given the choice between this world and a place by the side of God. There was a sense of heartache in the atmosphere. It was quite obvious that the day of separation was near. If religion had been completed, then the Prophet had also accomplished his mission. The eternal journey was inevitable since the mission had been fulfilled.

Overwhelmed by millions of thoughts and emotions, Abu Bakr sat in a corner and sobbed quietly.[87]

---

[87] *Sahih Muslim*, 4/1854 (2382)

THE TIME OF REUNION

The world was no place for an eternal friendship. The time for the Prophet to reunite with the Great Companion had arrived. As the time for his departure neared, the Prophet became ill. On one occasion, he fell unconscious. As he regained consciousness, he said: "Command Bilal to call the *adhan*! Command Abu Bakr to lead the prayer!"

Then the noble Messenger fell unconscious again. A short while later, he woke up and asked: "Have you performed the prayer?" This was an unusual situation, and they had not performed the prayer yet. Everyone was in shock as our mother, Aisha said: "My father is a softhearted man; he could not endure it. I wish that you had assigned someone else to this duty, oh noble Messenger of God!" As Aisha insisted, the noble Messenger became angry and raised his voice: "Command Bilal to call the Adhan! Command Abu Bakr to lead the prayer!"

It became obvious that this was a clear order that should not be questioned. The Prophet's command had to be fulfilled. Previously, the Prophet had also stated: "As long as Abu Bakr is amongst my people, it is not appropriate for someone else to lead the prayers."[88]

---

[88] *Sunanu'l-Beyhaki*, 8/152

Did not the Prophet indicate this before when he had ordered that all the doors to the Masjid be closed apart from the door that opened to Abu Bakr's home? The Prophet was not able to stay conscious for long periods of time anymore. Once again, he had lost consciousness, and when he came to, he asked whether the prayer had started.

This time, just as the Prophet had ordered, Abu Bakr was leading the prayer. The noble Prophet stood up with the aid of two Companions who supported him with their shoulders. With his feet dragging on the floor, he looked through the curtains. With his face that shone like the full moon, he watched his community for the last time. When he saw his appointed Imam standing in front, a radiant smile appeared on his noble face. Some of the people who saw him almost broke their prayers. He made a gesture, indicating that they should continue with their prayers. Then, he came up and stood by Abu Bakr's side. Abu Bakr tried to move behind him, but the Prophet did not give permission. This would be the last prayer that they performed together.[89] Finally, the curtains came down, never to be raised again...

Following the prayer, Abu Bakr assumed that the Prophet, peace and blessings be upon him, was feeling moderately better, and he went to visit his relatives that lived at the outskirts of Medina, a region called Sanah. At this time, the sun had set, and Mecca was blanketed with dark clouds.

Companions like Umar, who could not even think about the possibility of Prophet's departure from this world, had

---

[89] Nesai, *as-Sunanu'l-Kubra*, 1/280 (859)

drawn their swords. They were shouting: "I will have the head of any man who claims that he is dead!"[90]

They hoped that God's Messenger would return to them just as Moses did when he went to Mt. Sinai. For this reason, they were criticizing everyone who claimed that the Prophet was dead and accusing them of insincerity.

Eventually, a group of people came to Abu Bakr and explained to him what had happened. Abu Bakr was running like a gazelle. It was like he was flying through the air as the crowd opened the way for him.

When Abu Bakr stepped into the room, he looked so poignant that it seemed as if his body had folded in two. His heart was pounding so strongly that he felt as if it was about to burst out of his chest. He could not hold himself back anymore. He was hugging the Prophet's lifeless body. He lifted the piece of fabric off his radiant face and began to kiss his blessed forehead. Quickly, he placed his ear to the Prophet's mouth. He wanted to hear him breathe one last time, but there was no movement. Indeed, he was also a human being and just as all human beings, he too had to depart from this transient world one day. The noble Messenger had set sail towards eternity. In a physical sense, he was not with them anymore.

As usual, it was up to Abu Bakr to take control of the chaotic situation. Ever since the early days, when others panicked in certain unexpected situations, it was Abu Bakr who had to calm them down. This day, however, was

---

[90] Hayseme, *Majmau'z-Zawaed*, 9/38

quite an extraordinary day. Once again, all expectations were on Abu Bakr. He glanced at the body of the noble Messenger and said:

> May my mother and father be sacrificed to you! Just as you were beautiful in life, so are you beautiful in death! Nevertheless, you have also tasted the death, which was written by God![91]

Then, Abu Bakr made the following statement which reflected an interpretation of a verse from the holy Qur'an: "You will surely die (one day), and surely they (too) will die."[92]

The confused expressions on the faces of the Companions were directed at Abu Bakr. They asked: "Oh the defender of the Messenger of God! Did the Prophet really die?" Abu Bakr nodded with grief and then said: "Yes!"

Abu Bakr represented the truth. The luminous sun that had brightened their world and the afterworld had set. They continued with their questions: "Oh beloved friend of the Messenger of God! Is there a funeral prayer for Prophets?" Yes! replied Abu Bakr, and then told them to come in groups for the funeral prayer.

He was describing everything in detail to them. Step by step, Abu Bakr explained what needed to be done. They had so much confidence in him that they followed his instructions to the smallest details. They asked a question at each phase of the service. "Oh, beloved friend of the

---

[91] *Sahih Bukhari*, 3/1341 (3467)
[92] *Qur'an*, Surah Zumer: 39/30

Messenger of God! Do we bury the Prophet?" "Yes! replied, Abu Bakr without the slightest hesitation."

Once again, they asked: "Where do we bury him?" "On the spot that God collected his soul," replied Abu Bakr, who then continued: "Certainly, God has collected his soul at a clean and pure location."

However, explaining these issues to a few individuals was not enough. It was his duty to inform everyone. Abu Bakr came into the Masjid and spoke: "Oh people! Listen to me and listen well! Whoever serves Muhammad, should know that he is dead! But whoever serves God with sincerity, should know that He is eternal! Abu Bakr completed his speech by reciting the following Qur'anic verse:

> Muhammad is but a Messenger, and Messengers passed away before him. If, then, he dies or is killed, will you turn back on your heels? Whoever turns back on his heels can in no way harm God. But God will (abundantly) reward the thankful ones (those who are steadfast in God's cause).[93]

As Abu Bakr recited the verse, many of the Companions who were present, listened as if they were hearing the verse for the first time.[94] Perhaps, this was a verse that they had recited many times during their prayers or when they read the Qur'an.

---

[93] *Qur'an*, Ali Imran 3:144
[94] *Sahih Ibn Hebban*, 14/589 (6620)

ROAD TO CALIPHATE

Meanwhile, the Ashab and the Ansar had gathered to discuss to whom they would make their pledge after the noble Prophet. At first, they concentrated on the notion of a leader from each group. However, an intelligent mind like Umar realized that this would have led to confusion and conflict amongst the people. Umar knew that once two swords were drawn, they would have never returned to their sheaths. He convinced the group that there should only be one leader.

Abu Bakr was insistently invited to the meeting. As soon as he joined the meeting, Umar stood up and said:

> Oh the people of Ansar! Do you not know that the Messenger of God ordered Abu Bakr to lead the prayers? Would any of us enjoy stepping in front of Abu Bakr or pulling him down from a rank that the noble Messenger himself had designated for him?

Umar was addressing a group of righteous men. Therefore, they replied in coherence: "We seek refuge in God, from stepping in front of Abu Bakr, and beseech the Lord's mercy."[95]

---

[95] Hakim, *Mustadrak*, 3/70 (4423)

It was a confounding situation; on one side, there was the body of the noble Messenger who had walked towards God, and on the other, there was a discussion about who would fill his spot as the new leader. Indeed, on the one hand, there was the sorrow of the Prophet's departure, and on the other, a challenge to sail the ship through turbulent waters. The ship of Islam had to be sailed towards the safety of peaceful shores, and this had to be done without causing damage to the spirit of religion. Evidently, in those days, extreme care needed to be taken in order to avoid confusion. The empty seat of leadership had to be occupied by someone who was qualified. Otherwise, it would be filled by unqualified individuals.

Abu Bakr was surprised by the conversation. He attempted to intervene by arguing that the seat of leadership should be filled by an expert such as Umar or Abu Ubada. However, Umar Ibn al-Khattab was too quick for him. He spoke with authority: "Let me ask you this," argued Umar, who then continued: *"The second of the two when they were in the cave, and he said to his companion: 'Do not grieve. God is surely with us.'* (Tawba 9:40) Who is mentioned in this verse? Who was the person who was honored with the noble companionship?"

At this point, there were other voices supporting Umar: "How could we make our pledge to someone else when there is a Siddiq, the second of the two, amongst us?" In addition to this, the noble Messenger's words regarding guidance remained fresh in their minds: "The two individuals you should emulate after me are Abu Bakr and Umar."[96]

By this point in the discussion, they were all thinking about the same thing. They had dealt with possible conflicts quite swiftly. All issues had been solved on the same day and before nightfall. Finally, Umar grabbed Abu Bakr's hand and placed it on top of his own. This was an indication that the noble Messenger's first caliph had been elected. Following Umar, they all came and made their pledges to Abu Bakr. This was the beginning of a challenging episode for Abu Bakr. He was a caliph now…the Caliph of the noble Messenger of God and all the believers.

Following the pledge, Abu Bakr climbed to the minbar (pulpit in a mosque). This was the Minbar from which the noble Prophet used to deliver his sermons. As Abu Bakr climbed the Minbar, he was on his toes. He had great respect for the Prophet's memories. He stopped half way through the steps and began to address the people. This was Abu Bakr's first sermon. He spoke with a soft, tender voice:

> Oh people! You have chosen me as your leader although I am not the most blessed amongst you. For this reason, help and support me when I do the right thing, and invite me to the right path when I sway away from it. Without doubt, righteousness is an entrusted gift and dishonesty is a form of treachery. I hope to God that the weakest person amongst you will be the strongest person when I protect his rights. And the strongest person amongst you will be

---

[96] *Sunanu't-Tirmidhi*, 5/609 (3662)

> the weakest when I correct his wrongs. Beware, none of you should stand back from struggling on the path of God. Remember, those who displayed negligence in this regard. They have all been slapped with degradation by God. God will send great calamities upon societies where adultery is freely spread. Obey me, so long as I obey God. However, do not obey me, if I make an error in submission to my God and the noble Messenger.[97]

The owner of these words was a man who would bring down the kingdoms of Persia and Byzantium. High rank and position had only increased his modesty. Abu Bakr had become more sensitive with the weight of the Prophet's people resting on his shoulders. According to Abu Bakr, power was not given so that it could be used for oppression. On the contrary, it was a burden that needed to be carried and a duty that had to be fulfilled.

Abu Bakr was an extremely sensitive man; however, he was also a genius who would establish an incredible system at a time when the foundations of society began to make a cracking noise. His accomplishment would be hailed with a great praise from Umar who became the second Caliph following Abu Bakr. According to Umar's testimony, Abu Bakr left behind a very comfortable path to those who came after.

---

[97] Ibn Hisham, *as-Siratu'n-Nabawiyya*, 6/82

FUTILE OPPOSITION

Of course, some decided to fish in murky waters. Some people who were disappointed by Abu Bakr's election as the Caliph had already commenced to search for an alternative. A small group went to Ali and said: "How could we leave this duty in the hands of the weakest individuals of the Quraysh?"[98]

In order to strengthen the opposition, they were looking for support. Influential personalities such as Ali were important in challenging the Caliphate of Abu Bakr. They were desperately trying to draw Ali's attention. One instigator came to Ali and said: "Just say the word and I will invade Medina with a large army consisting of horsemen and foot soldiers. I will support you to the end."[99]

All of these seditions had one objective and that was to bring down Islam using the internal sources. Certainly, they had to be dealt with. Upon listening to all proposals and suggestions, Ali took control over the situation and said: "We have found Abu Bakr to be the appropriate person for this job."[100] With his statement, Ali was closing all doors that led to seditions and conflicts.

---

[98] Tabari, *Tarihu't-Tabari*, 2/237
[99] Tabari, *Tarihu't-Tabari*, 2/237
[100] Tabari, *Tarihu't-Tabari*, 2/237

On another occasion, when Ali was approached with similar proposals, he felt so frustrated that he replied sternly with the following statement:

> The Messenger of God ordered Abu Bakr to lead the prayers! I was not absent, I was amongst them! I was not ill either, I was healthy! If he wished that I lead the prayer, he would have ordered it! From a religious perspective, God and His noble Messenger were pleased with him, so from a worldly perspective, we should also be pleased with him.[101]

This statement was an indication that all doors were finally closed for those who still carried the opposition bug. Following the statement, Ali came to Abu Bakr and made his pledge.

---

[101] Abu Ja'far et-Tabari, *er-Riyadu'n-Nadera*, 2/177

HIS ATTITUDE TOWARDS INHERITORS

The noble Messenger's daughter Fatima and his uncle Abbas came to the Caliph and requested their inheritance. There was a small piece of land that belonged to the Prophet, and they had a share in this land. However, this was when the Prophet was still alive.

Abu Bakr loved everyone whom the noble Messenger of God loved. If requested, he would have given everything he possessed to them. However, this was a religious matter that needed to be solved according to religious rulings. Religious rulings stated that Prophets did not leave inheritance; their belongings were regarded as charity. Abu Bakr had heard this from the noble Messenger himself; therefore, he declined their request without hesitation.[102]

Later on, he requested information about this saying of the Prophet from Umar, Talha, Zubayr, Sa'd Ibn Waqqas, and Abdurrahman Ibn Awf. These important individuals agreed with Abu Bakr. It was evident that the noble Messenger of God did not have beneficiaries.

Since being a beneficiary was out of the question, Fatima inquired about the possibility of donation. She said to Abu

---

[102] *Sahih Muslim*, 3/1381 (1759)

Bakr: "You know that when the Messenger of God was alive, he donated this land to me. This makes me a gift bearer not a beneficiary." Abu Bakr replied with an argument:

> Yes, I am aware of this. However, the noble Messenger gave you a certain share that was sufficient for your needs. I have seen him distribute the remaining portion to those in poverty. This means that those in need have continuous rights over the land.

The issue was not solved yet, so Fatima came up with another solution: "If that is the case, then let us keep the land and benefit from it just as the way we used to do during the Prophet's time." Abu Bakr replied to this proposal with the following reasoning:

> I do not believe that this is the right solution either. After the noble Prophet, it is my duty to handle the issues faced by the believers. I have more rights over this than you, so I shall take control and make sure that it is distributed the way it was done during the time of the Prophet.[103]

Obviously, this was not a trust problem. Those who were close to the noble Prophet had a unique place by the side of Abu Bakr. However, this was a social issue that needed to be addressed through religious rulings and principles. The rights of the society had to be protected. Otherwise, religious rulings would be altered according to individuals, and eventually, there would be no rulings left in the name of religion.

---

[103] *Sahih Bukhari*, 3/1126 (2926)

HEJAZ SHAKEN WITH CONTROVERSY

According to the testimony of Abu Bakr's daughter Aisha, the mother of believers, the burdens and troubles placed on Abu Bakr's shoulders along with the duty of Caliphate were so heavy that if they were placed on mountain tops, they would have been crushed and crumbled to pieces.[104]

The noble Prophet's departure from this transient world was a great opportunity for devious minds that began to declare their Prophethood. There were false prophets appearing all over the region of Hejaz. There were also people who had not submitted to Islam in a complete sense. Although they were performing their prayers, they declined to give zakat (an obligatory alms giving). New religious perspectives had emerged, and conflicts between different ethnic groups began to erupt. The ambiance was engulfed with conflicts and seditions. Even on the first day of the Prophet's departure, there were rumors about Usama's army prepared by the noble Messenger himself. The foundations of unity were shaking with rumors and seditions.

---

[104] Ibn Kesr, *el-Bidaya wa'n-Nihaya*, 6/304

Nevertheless, Abu Bakr was the right man for the job. It was divine destiny. The Almighty God had granted Abu Bakr a place by the side of the Prophet, where he would be prepared for difficult times like this. Abu Bakr was blessed with the potential to establish a solid system that would protect the unity of Islam, following the Prophet's departure. This was so evident that many years later, Umar would be compelled to make the following statement:

> I have seen that Abu Bakr's staunch approach to the issues of rebellion and upheaval was more imposing than mine. During his Caliphate, he had succeeded in teaching people the ethics of Islam, so much so that I had no difficulties in administration during my Caliphate.

Ibn Masud also honored Abu Bakr with the following words:

> After the noble Messenger of God, we had to deal with so many troublesome incidents. If God had not granted us a leader like Abu Bakr, we would have been destroyed.[105]

---

[105] Khaled Muhammad, *we Jae Abu Bakr*, 89

DETERRENT SOLUTION TO ZAKAT VIOLATION

There were those who used the Prophet's departure as an excuse to avoid paying their Zakat. Although, these people continued to perform their prayers, their greed for wealth had turned them away from Zakat. They declared that they would no longer give the obligatory alms. Perhaps, they were not arguing against the fact that Zakat was an obligatory act, but they were claiming that there was no need for it anymore because the Prophet had passed away.

With his shrewdness, Abu Bakr quickly realized what lied beyond this disease that threatened the society. The smallest concession given here would have opened the way for many other requests, and in turn, the people of Islam would have fallen apart, even more rapidly than those before them. For this reason, Abu Bakr was ever determined as he declared war against these people. Companions like Umar argued: "How could you declare war against people who bear witness that God is one and Muhammad is His Messenger?" Abu Bakr announced:

"Even if it is a simple halter, if it was collected during the time of the Prophet then I shall also collect it."[106]

With his firm stance, Abu Bakr prevented the collapse of unity. Even some of his close friends who tried to warn him at the beginning were now beginning to understand the reason for his determination. They were coming to Abu Bakr and admitting to the fact that they were in the wrong. Comparions such as Abu Hurayra, who had witnessed Abu Bakr's determination during difficult times, praised him with the following statement: "If it wasn't for Abu Bakr, we would have fallen into chaos. We would not have established order ever again."[107]

---

[106] *Sahih Muslim*, 1/51(20)
[107] Abu Ja'far et-Tabari, *er-Riyadu'n-Nadera*, 2/47

INCIDENTS OF APOSTASY

A group of people whose beliefs were weak used this opportunity to gather at a location called Zu'l Kissa, situated out of Medina. There were also those who made the most of situations like this. Even rumors suggesting that these people were intending to declare war on Medina had reached the ears of Abu Bakr.

Abu Bakr wasted no time as he drew his sword and rode towards the location. He seemed so upset that he did not even notice those who stood on his path. Ali realized that this was not a good sign. Swiftly, he rode after Abu Bakr and caught up with him. Ali grabbed Abu Bakr's mount by the reins and shouted with anger:

> Where are you going, oh the Caliph of the noble Messenger! I wish to remind you of the words that the noble Messenger said to you on the day of Uhud: "Do not put us in grief by throwing yourself into danger!" I swear by God, if something happens to you today, no longer there will be order and harmony, in the name of Islam![108]

---

[108] Abu Ja'far et-Tabari, *er-Riyadu'n-Nadera*, 2/46

FALSE PROPHETS

The medium was suitable for the breeding of deceitful instigators. Some were claiming to be prophets, and that they were the rightful owner of the leadership. A man called Tuhayla claimed that he was a prophet. He belonged to the clan of Asad where he found plenty of support. Before long, his influence had reached all the way to the son of Amir, Hawazan, and Sulaym. Many people with character disorders had joined his movement.

A short while later, a woman named Sajah from the sons of Tamim, also claimed that she was a prophet. However, the loudest voice came from Yamama. A man called Musaylima declared his prophethood and claimed that he was receiving revelations. Musaylima was a man made up of nothing but egotism. He had even fabricated some gibberish which he conveyed as revelations. The sad thing about the entire incident was that he had found a significant number of followers. These people resembled an evil chorus that frequently chanted: "We obeyed the Messenger of God for as long as he was amongst us. However, after the Prophet's departure, we will not comply with Abu Bakr or any other servant of God."[109]

---

[109] Khaled Muhammad, *wa Jae Abu Bakr*, 94

They would listen to nothing but their own egos. However, there were those who had total submission in God. They would not stand aside and watch these false claims destroy the very fabric of society. Abu Bakr was one of these valiant souls. Quickly, he prepared armies and dispatched them to every snake hole for decontamination.

Abu Bakr and his armies were quite determined, and this was enough to convince many who fled hastily from the scene. Before long, this problem would also be solved, and breeding grounds for these problematic characters who claimed prophethood would be sterilized.

USAMA'S ARMY

Abu Bakr was elected as the new Caliph, but there was an army that had been waiting for his orders for quite some time now. This army was prepared by the noble Messenger of God when he was still alive. He had chosen Usama as the commander of the large army. Usama was only twenty eight at the time. It was evident that the noble Messenger wished to take the banner of God to the four corners of the world even though he was about to bid farewell to this world. This was a physical prayer offered by the Prophet who wanted to spread the religion of God to every location upon which the sun rose. The name selected for the job indicated that this sanctified objective could only be achieved with a valiant soul like Usama.

The mission given to this army was evident. They would march towards those who had martyred Usama's father, Zaid, at the battle of Muta.

Some approached Abu Bakr, arguing that the military expedition should be postponed because people were still in mourning the death of the Prophet. Some claimed that the army should remain in Medina to deal with insubordination.[110]

---

[110] Tabari, *Tarihu't-Tabari*, 2/246

There were even those who argued that Usama was too young, and he was the son of an emancipated slave.[111] However, Abu Bakr was not about to hold back an army that was prepared by the noble Messenger of God, himself. He turned all of them down and said:

> Make way for Usama's army! I swear by God that if I was attacked by wolves and torn to pieces, I would still see this army off. I would not turn back on a decree given by the Messenger of God![112]

Indeed, the army that was prepared by the Messenger of God had to be sent, and the noble Messenger's wish had to be fulfilled.

They had convinced Umar, and using his influence, they wanted to express their concerns regarding Usama. According to them, Usama was too young and inexperienced. Amongst the soldiers, there were mature Companions who had experience in commandership. Umar had not completed his sentence yet when the usually calm and collected Abu Bakr jumped in like a roaring lion. He grabbed Umar by his beard and shouted: "Shame on you, oh son of Khattab! How could you ask me to remove him from command when the noble Messenger, himself, gave him this duty?"[113] Umar had no other alternative but to remain silent. Abu Bakr's willpower had closed another door that may have led to conflicts.

---

[111] Tabari, *Tarihu't-Tabari*, 2/246
[112] Tabari, *Tarihu't-Tabari*, 2/246
[113] Tabari, *Tarihu't-Tabari*, 2/246

Usama marched out of Medina with his army. Abu Bakr was on foot as he sent them off. Young Usama was experiencing the emotions of embarrassment and shock as the Caliph of the believers was on foot, walking besides him. He asked Abu Bakr to mount his horse, but Abu Bakr refused, gesturing with his hand: "By God, neither you will dismount nor will I mount your horse. Let my feet get dirty on the path of God, at least for awhile."[114]

Certainly, if Abu Bakr had not carried such a hefty load on his shoulders, he would have been a soldier in this army that was prepared by the noble Messenger of God. Indeed, the situations prevented him from going with the army, but the least he could do was to show that his heart was with them. Perhaps, walking besides them as they marched out of the city provided some consolation for Abu Bakr.

Abu Bakr had a small request for the young commander. He asked for permission to keep Umar in Medina. He needed Umar's support and help. He said: "If it is alright with you, I would like to keep Umar by my side, so that he could support me. Under these conditions, I see great benefit and blessing in having Umar by my side."

In actuality, Abu Bakr was the Caliph of the people and the Caliph of the commander that led the army. He could have made this decision without consulting anyone. Yet even under those difficult conditions, he asked for permission from the young commander to keep Umar in Medi-

---

[114] Tabari, *Tarihu't-Tabari*, 2/246

na. Moreover, he did this with the upmost sincerity. It was evident that if Usama had refused, Umar would have been forced to go with Usama's army.

However, Usama was raised in a home that was inundated with tranquility. He would certainly comply with the Caliph's request, and he did so with modesty.

The time of parting had arrived. However, the soldiers had expectations from the Caliph. They wanted advice and instructions regarding the strategy and objectives of the battle. Abu Bakr paused for a few moments and then shouted:

> Oh people! Stand where you are and listen to the following ten recommendations:
>
> Do not betray.
>
> Do not deceive anyone.
>
> Do not treat anyone unjustly.
>
> Respect the dead and do not mutilate their corpses.
>
> Do not kill their women, children, and the elders.
>
> Do not chop their trees down.
>
> Do not harm their crops.
>
> Do not slaughter sheep, cattle, or camels unless you need it for food.
>
> If you come across people who have dedicated themselves to worship and prayer; leave them alone and do not pester them.
>
> You may also come across people who will offer food to you in different bowls and varieties; do not eat before mentioning the name of God.

Abu Bakr completed his speech with the following statement:

> You will run into people who will appear as if they were on your side, yet they will look for ways to overpower you and will plan your demise. These are the people you should fight to the end!

Abu Bakr had finalized his recommendations, and it was time to bid farewell. First he said: "Go on and begin your journey with the name of God!" Then he offered the following prayer: "May God protect you from the tyranny of the enemy and from the plague!"[115]

This was the difference between an average human being and a person who was trained by the side of the noble Prophet. Even in war, he set the rules of engagement. Human beings had to be treated justly, as human beings. Even on the battlefield, there were rules and these rules were set by religious decrees, not by human emotions, such as hatred, hostility, egotism, and arrogance. Today, those who follow the principles of modern humanitarians should realize how distant they still are from Abu Bakr's horizon. Finally, Abu Bakr waved goodbye to the army of the noble Messenger of God and returned to Medina to deal with the conflicts that shuddered the region of Hejaz.

---

[115] Tabari, *Tarihu't-Tabari*, 2/246

PEACE AND SERENITY

In a short period of time, those who competed with each other in a race of insurgency were contained. In a sense, order had been established. From that point on, Abu Bakr planned to accomplish certain objectives that he had scheduled on short and long term basis. These objectives consisted of targets shown by the noble Messenger of God. Abu Bakr reserved all of his resources and energy to this cause as he worked vigorously throughout the days and the nights.

Without doubt, his biggest support was Umar Ibn al-Khattab. Abu Bakr assigned Umar to judicial duties. Conflicts and disputes that erupted amongst the citizens of Medina were brought before Umar. Justice was Umar's business as he lived and breathed justice. Umar's sensitivity towards justice had earned him the title of "Faruq," which carried the meaning of "the separator of truth and falsehood."

It was about a year after Umar's appointment. He came to the Caliph and requested to be removed from this duty. Obviously, there was a reason, so Abu Bakr questioned the reason behind his request. Umar's reply was quite interesting. He complained that since his appointment to judge duties, a year ago, not even two people had come to him requesting for a resolution regarding a dispute.[116]

Umar's testimony also showed that people who were sincerely committed to serving God and His noble Messenger did not face significant problems in their society. The reason for this was they lived in the most blessed century of all and were about to enter into the second most blessed century. The Messenger of God, peace and blessing be upon him, had once stated: "The most blessed of all human beings are the ones that live in the century that I live, followed by the one after…and the one after."[117]

---

[116] Muhammad Sabit, *Abu Bakr as-Siddiq*, 96
[117] *Sahih Muslim*, 4/1962 (2533)

FINANCIAL HARDSHIP

In the early days of Abu Bakr's Caliphate, Umar Ibn al-Khattab and Abu Ubayda were on their way to Abu Bakr's house to pay a visit. On the way, they saw a person carrying a roll of material on his shoulders. He was wearing old clothes. At first, they had never suspected it, but suddenly they heard a voice greeting them, "may God's peace be upon you." This was the voice of Abu Bakr. In shock, they asked: "Oh the Caliph of the noble Messenger. Where are you going?" Abu Bakr replied with a low tone of voice: "To the marketplace."

Evidently, Abu Bakr, once a renowned businessman, was trying to earn a living for his family. His aim was to sell the roll of material that he carried on his shoulders. Umar raised his voice: "What business do you have at the market when the entire load of the Muslims is already on your shoulders!?" Abu Bakr made a gesture, indicating that they should move out of his way. Then he said: "How will I feed my children?" Umar took control of the situation, using his judicious mind: "Come with us! We will arrange a salary for you, from the treasury department."

Umar quickly summoned all the prominent Companions to the mosque. First, he explained the situation to them and then expressed his views on the matter. They were all thinking along the same lines as Umar. Therefore, they decided on a certain amount of salary so that Abu Bakr could spend all of his time dealing with the issues of the believers.[118]

Before he became a Caliph, Abu Bakr had certain habits which he had turned into customary duties. He ran to the aid of the needy, prepared dough for the orphans, and performed chores for those who could not do them anymore. One of the chores he performed was milking their sheep. He was helping widows whose husbands were martyred in battles and orphans who had no financial support.

In contrast to the new problems that were arising in the Hejaz, Abu Bakr continued to knock on the doors of the needy. As he knocked on one door, the little girl of the house opened it. Upon seeing Abu Bakr standing there, she shouted: "Mum! That man who milks our sheep is here!"

The old women rushed to the door and came face to face with Abu Bakr. She felt extremely mortified. Quickly, she turned towards her daughter and shouted with a questioning tone of voice: "Shame on you! Listen to yourself, how could you talk about the Caliph of the Prophet in such manner?"

Some other members of this particular clan who had heard about Abu Bakr's appointment were wondering who would perform their chores now. However, Abu

---

[118] Khaled Muhammad, *wa Jae Abu Bakr*, 110

Bakr was a kind of man and would prove them wrong. The Caliph approached the crowd and said: "Yes, I will continue to milk your sheep. I hope that my position will not discourage me from my customs."[119]

Following the incident, Abu Bakr continued to milk their sheep for a year. He was so modest that during the milking process, he followed the instructions given by the shepherd that looked after the herd. Abu Bakr, the Caliph of the Prophet, did not even turn this into an issue about pride and honor.[120]

---

[119] Ibn Sa'd, *Tabaqatu'l-Kubra*, 3/186
[120] Ibn Sa'd, *Tabaqatu'l-Kubra*, 3/186

PIETY AND FEAR OF GOD

No one could question his piety and fear of God. The only concern he had in life was the one regarding his cause. He used all his means on this path. Worldly features such as wealth, nobility and rank had no value in his eyes. They could never change Abu Bakr, and they never did.

On one occasion, he felt extremely thirsty, so they brought him a cup of water. They served the water with a small portion of honey. As he was about to raise the cup to his mouth, he withdrew and began to weep. He was weeping so deeply that those present also began to weep. A short while later, everyone stopped except for Abu Bakr, who continued to weep loudly. There were those who feared the Caliph would die of suffocation. In fact, this was the best way of being an example. He was teaching a lesson through actions. Finally, Abu Bakr regained his composure. They asked: "Oh the Caliph of the noble Messenger of God! What made you weep so much?" He tried to reply, as he continued to sob: One day, I was sitting with the Prophet. He was pushing something away with his hands. I could not see what it was, so I asked: "Oh noble Messenger of God! What is that you try to push away, I could not see anyone there?" He replied:

> That is the world. It appeared before me. I said, be gone and sent it away. It went away only to return once again to say:
>
> "Even if you succeed in sending me away, those after you will not succeed."

At this point, Abu Bakr explained as to why he had wept; "I remembered this incident and feared that the world had found acceptance in me. This is why I wept."[121]

Although he possessed the mentality to endure all types of hardship and difficulties, sometimes he wished to be alone with nature. These were the times when he felt a bit dejected. On one of these melancholic days, he saw a bird alone flying freely above the trees. It was singing songs of freedom as it flew from one branch to another. For awhile, he watched in great amazement. Then, he made the following statement:

> Joy be to you! How I wish that I could be like you! How I wish to be a bird that has no accountability and punishment. I wish I could land on different branches, feed myself from the tree, and fly away.[122]

On another occasion, when he was feeling the weight of the hefty load on his shoulders, he noticed a tree. He said: "I wish that I was a timber that would be chopped off and disposed of."[123]

He did not like to be praised. Whenever he faced such a situation, he would open his hands and pray: "Oh Lord!

---

[121] Abu Ja'far et-Tabari, *er-Riyadu'n-Nadera*, 2/136
[122] Bayhaki, *Shuabu'l-Iman*, 1/485 (788)
[123] Bayhaki, *Shuabu'l-Iman*, 1/485 (788)

You know me better than I know myself. However, I know myself better than these people. Make me into a person who deserves these praises. Forgive me for the things they do not know. Do not hold me accountable for what they say."[124]

Those who believed that Abu Bakr was extremely sensitive about these issues reminded him of all the joyful tidings that the noble Messenger brought in regards to him. Still he was never certain of himself. He replied: "I swear by God! Even if I found myself with both legs stretched in paradise, I would not be certain of its justification."[125]

Competing in a race for good was in their nature, and this quality was not restricted to Abu Bakr. Umar Ibn al-Khattab had assigned a duty for himself; he would perform chores for a blind old woman who lived at the outskirts of Medina. He would drop by her house on regular basis to ask if she needed anything. Whenever he visited her, she would tell him that someone else had already attended to her needs.

Umar was curious about this person who always beat him to the punch. On each visit, Umar tried to come at an earlier time to meet the other person. However, he was always there before him. Later on, he realized that it was Abu Bakr who visited the old woman.

Earning his living through lawful means was extremely important for Abu Bakr. He would have easily risked his life not to allow a morsel of *haram* food not to go through his mouth.

---

[124] Ibnu'l-Esr, *Usudu'l-Gabe*, 3/324
[125] Khaled Muhammad, *wa Jae Abu Bakr*, 113

One day, a servant offered Abu Bakr a plate of food. Abu Bakr consumed the food. Later on, the servant asked Abu Bakr: "Oh the Caliph of the noble Messenger! Do you know where this food came from?" In a matter of seconds, Abu Bakr was drenched in sweat as he trembled with fear. Obviously, the servant knew something. Abu Bakr asked with trepidation: "Where did it come from?" The servant repented for having asked, but he could not lie to Abu Bakr. There was no other option but to explain everything in detail:

> During the era of ignorance, there was a man who asked me to tell his fortune. I was not a good fortune teller, so I deceived him. Today, I ran into him, and he gave me the money he owed. The food you ate was purchased with that money.

Before the servant completed his sentence, Abu Bakr had his finger in his mouth. He was desperately trying to throw up. He wanted to vomit everything he had consumed. A person who noticed Abu Bakr's desperation, said: "May God have mercy on you! Are you doing this just for a morsel of food?" The Caliph of believers replied:

> I swear by God! In order to throw up all the food I had consumed, I would have risked my life because once I heard the noble Messenger say:
>
> "Hellfire is better for bodies that are nourished with *haram* and the forbidden." I feared the risk of being nourished with this food, and this is why I threw up everything.[126]

---

[126] Abu Nuaym el-Isbahani, *Hilyetu'l-Awliya*, 1/31

REUNION WITH UMMU AYMAN

The noble Prophet was a symbol of faithfulness, and he encouraged his followers to behave in the same manner. He recurrently visited his nanny, Ummu Ayman, when he was alive.

Without doubt, Abu Bakr was amongst those who followed this Prophetic tradition. Besides his daily duties, when he had time for himself, he would ask Umar to accompany him on a visit to Ummu Ayman. On one of these occasions, they came to the home of Ummu Ayman. She began to cry, upon seeing the Caliph of the Prophet and his number one supporter in her house. She could not hold her emotions, realizing that these two faithful men had left their important duties aside to pay her a visit. Moreover, they reminded her of the noble Prophet, peace and blessings be upon him. They asked: "Why do you weep? Certainly, being by the side of God is more blessed for the noble Messenger!" They tried to comfort her, but she continued to cry for awhile. A few minutes later, she wiped her tears away and replied: "I know that being by the side of God is more blessed for the noble Messenger! I do not weep for him. I weep because heavens have stopped sending down the divine revelations." How could such sensitivity hold Abu Bakr and Umar back? They joined Ummu Ayman and began to weep together.[127]

Abu Bakr conveyed the truth without any hesitation, and at every opportunity he found, he informed people and cautioned them about the principles of religion. One day he noticed two people talking about the principles of religion in a vigorous manner. One of them claimed that one should perform all the religious obligations but should not be concerned with the actions of others. He was supporting his claim with a verse from the holy Qur'an.

A religiously sensitive man, like Abu Bakr could not have ignored such a conversation involving a Qur'anic interpretation. However, he did not wish to restrict the issue to a small group. He wanted to analyze the matter with the entire community. First, he led the noon prayer and then turned towards the congregation, explaining:

> Oh people! There is a verse that you misunderstand and misinterpret:
> "O you who believe! Your responsibility is your selves (so consider how you are faring along your own way). Those who go astray can do you no harm if you yourselves are rightly guided."

Abu Bakr was focusing on this particular verse because he had heard one of the men argue that if one performed his prayers, observed the fast, and gave alms, those who refrained from these obligations were not his concern. The man's claim suggested that he was against the notion of

---
[127] *Sahih Muslim*, 4/1907 (2454)

inviting people towards good and forbidding them from sin. This was an example of interpreting God's message according to one's own carnal desires. No one had the right to do this. Inviting people towards good and forbidding them from sins was a social obligation. If abandoned, it could have had serious impact on society. For this reason, Abu Bakr continued to deliver his speech with words he had heard from the noble Messenger of God and said that if human beings come across a tyrant and do not make an effort to stop him, they should fear God's punishment that may come upon the entire society. "Then they raise their hands to beg for forgiveness. However, God does not accept their pleas then."[128]

---

[128] Ahmed b. Hanbal, *Musnad*, 1/7 (29)

TWO YEARS OF PROFUSE BLESSINGS

Within a short period of two years as Caliph, Abu Bakr tackled extremely complicated issues and established principles that would be easily implemented by those who came after him. Abu Bakr's achievements reflected the mind of a genius who would bid farewell to this world upon the completion of his mission. Not only he had solved many internal issues, but he put his signature underneath many victories that enabled the spreading of Islam to the entire world.

One of Abu Bakr's significant achievements was preserving the holy Qur'an into a book format. He had such great concerns regarding the martyring of Hafizes (people who memorized the entire Quran) that he consulted Umar about preserving the Qur'an in a book format. Abu Bakr achieved this with Umar's support.

As a result of the many battles that took place all around the region, Iraq was conquered by the Muslims, Iran had been forced to compromise, the region of Damascus was included into Islamic territories, and the Byzantine Empire was shaken from its foundations. All of these achievements were squeezed into two years. In those days, Byzantium and the Persian Empire were the superpowers of the world, and no one possessed the courage to confront them until Abu Bakr came to power.

AS THE CURTAINS COME DOWN

Separation from God's Messenger, with whom he had spent much of his life, had taken its toll on Abu Bakr. It was just over two years since the Prophet had passed away. As destiny would have it, Abu Bakr followed the tradition of his beloved friend. For this to occur, he needed to reach the age of sixty-three.

He was bed-stricken with illnesses.[129] As he prepared to set sail towards his last journey, his friends visited him by his bedside. When they realized the severity of his illness, they said:

"Oh the Caliph of the noble Messenger! Let us summon a doctor for you." Abu Bakr was cautious as he replied: "I have already consulted a doctor."

"What did he say to you? they asked.

"I do whatever I wish, in a way I decide," replied Abu Bakr. [130]

It was obvious that he had received his invitation, and the time to go had arrived. He called his daughter, Aisha, the mother of believers and instructed her to return the

---

[129] According to some reports, he fell ill due to food poisoning. Look up: Abu Ja'far et-Tabari, *er-Riyadu'n-Nadera*, 2/243
[130] Ibn Sa'd, *Tabaqatu'l-Kubra*, 3/198

remaining amount of his salary back to the treasury department. He also had a dying wish. He wanted to be buried next to his beloved friend whom he had never left throughout his life. He asked them to abstain from ostentatious ceremonies and instructed them to use his old clothes as the winding sheet. It was his will that his wife Asma, the daughter of Umays, wash his body with his son Abdurrahman.

Just like the noble Messenger, as Abu Bakr approached the time of separation, he instructed Umar to lead the prayers. He had nominated the person who would be the next Caliph.[131]

Umar would also lead his last prayer.[132] Abu Bakr, the great Caliph had lived such a responsive life that he took extreme care in refraining from spending the salary they had allocated to him contrary to his persistent refusals. As soon as he realized that death was knocking on his door, he displayed signs of apprehension. He remembered the amount he had been saving. Quickly, he summoned his relatives and told them to return the amount he had saved back to the treasury department. He had only used a small portion of the salary for fundamental necessities. He said to them:

"Umar did not let me be, and I had to take six thousands dirhams from the treasury. This amount is con-

---

[131] Abu Ja'far et-Tabari, *er-Riyadu'n-Nadera*, 2/242
[132] Abu Ja'far et-Tabari, *er-Riyadu'n-Nadera*, 2/241

cealed on a wall at such location. Take the money and return it to Umar."[133]

Then, Abu Bakr summoned Aisha, the mother of believers and spoke to her. With difficulty, he tried to speak:

> Since I have taken on the duties of serving the Muslims, I have not spent a dirham or a dinar of their money. On the contrary, I lived as the poorest person amongst them. I wore old clothes and experienced hunger on many occasions. All I have next to me is this piece of fabric and this servant, and they belong to the treasury. Take them to Umar.[134]

Following Abu Bakr's death, Umar took a long stare at the servant and the piece of garment that was brought before him and said: "May God have mercy on you, oh Abu Bakr! You have left a difficult life to follow for those who remain here.[135]

Abu Bakr's daughter Aisha explained her father's last journey with the following words:

> When my father fell unconscious with the severity of his illness, I recited a poem: "No matter how much a person tries to conceal her tears, they will most certainly flow out one day." When my father regained his consciousness, he said: "Do not say that, my dear baby! You should recite the verse: And the stupor of death comes in truth (being the established decree of

---

[133] Ibn Sa'd, *Tabaqatu'l-Kubra*, 3/193
[134] Ibn Sa'd, *Tabaqatu'l-Kubra*, 3/196
[135] Ibn Sa'd, *Tabaqatu'l-Kubra*, 3/196

God for life). That is, (O human) what you were trying to escape (Qaf 50:19).

And then, he asked:

"On which day did the noble Messenger pass away?"

"It was Monday," I replied. He continued with his questions:

"What day is it today?"

"Monday!" When he heard my reply, he said:

"I hope to God that I do not see another night after this one!"

Once again, he asked:

"How many winding sheets was he wrapped in?"

"We wrapped him in three white garments of Sahulliyah! He did not have a shirt or a turban."

Then he said:

"Wash my garment! There is a stain on it, and then add two more garments to it."

I was about to say that the garment was worn out, when he intervened:

It does not matter. The living need new clothes more than the dead. Moreover, a dead person's shroud will decay rapidly.[136]

On that particular day, Abu Bakr flew towards the exalted souls. He had died on the same day and at the same age as the noble Messenger of God. The age difference between the Prophet and Abu Bakr was compensated through the two years of Caliphate. Abu Bakr's last words were: "Oh Lord, take my soul to You as a Muslim,

---

[136] Abu Ja'far et-Tabari, *er-Riyadu'n-Nadera*, 2/240

and join me with the righteous."[137] This was the prayer of Prophet Joseph, who lived the joy of reunion following a life of torments.

Medina was in tears upon the news of his death. The region of Hejaz was living a day similar to the day that the noble Prophet had passed away. Upon hearing the news, Ali burst into tears and rushed to Abu Bakr's house. He showed great respect as he stood by Abu Bakr's body. He said:

May God have mercy on you, oh Abu Bakr! You were the leading figure of Islam, the most perfect example of faith, a person who feared God the most and carried the heaviest load out of all human beings. In following the Prophet, no one could show more sincerity than you and no one could be more sensitive towards their friends.[138]

---

[137] Abu Ja'far et-Tabari, *er-Riyadu'n-Nadera*, 2/242
[138] Hayseme, *Majmau'z-Zawaed*, 9/48

HIS INHERITANCE

A man who was once the prominent businessmen of Mecca, and a person who the Quraysh respected with veneration, Abu Bakr, the Caliph of the noble Messenger, had left behind a camel for milking, a servant, and a cup used for milking.[139] This was all that was left for his beneficiaries. However, the title "Abu Bakr the Truthful" was a wealth that the inhabitants of the earth could never attain until the Day of Judgment.

Once again, Abu Bakr had taken his place by the side of the noble Prophet, and Umar was the new Caliph and the second vizier. First of all, they brought Abu Bakr's possessions to Umar. There was a large clay jug that contained something. They had no other option but to break it, so that they could find out what was stored in it. As they broke the jug, the money it contained splattered all over the floor. Upon seeing this, Umar could not hold himself back anymore, and he spoke in tears: "May God have mercy on you, oh Abu Bakr! You did not leave a word for those who come after you. Now, I am the person taking on the responsibility of this duty."[140]

---

[139] Ibn Sa'd, *Tabaqatu'l-Kubra*, 3/196
[140] Abu Ja'far et-Tabari, *er-Riyadu'n-Nadera*, 2/245

This was a way that Umar called himself to account. Umar realized that he had to be extremely sensitive in taking over the position of a person who served with critical calculations that involved investigating the issues to the smallest detail. According to Umar, reaching such a level of sensitivity was almost impossible.

Following Abu Bakr's death, Umar visited his house and spoke to his wife, Asma Bint Umays. He asked her about Abu Bakr's religious practices on a personal level. She explained:

> He woke up before sunrise and performed Wudu. Then he began to perform his prayers. He prayed for so long! Then he recited the Qur'an and wept as he read. He would weep during the prostration and weep during the prayer. These were the times when I would detect a scent that smelled like a cooked liver.

As Umar listen to the words of grieving Asma, he became emotional. Umar was weeping with Asma as he said: "How could you compare yourself to such servanthood, oh the son of Khattab?!"

HIS FAMILY LIFE

Abu Bakr's family had certain qualities that no other family possessed. His family was the cause of the revelation of the verse that permitted Muslims to use the earth to take Wudu when there was no water. Following the revelation, Companions like Usayd Ibn Hudayr said, "Certainly, this is not the only blessing granted to the Abu Bakr family"[141]. Amongst the Companions, Abu Bakr's family was the only family that had the reputation of four generation of Muslims. This had been accomplished both through Abdurrahman and Asma.

As it is known, Abu Bakr was married for four times, and through his marriages that occurred at different times, he had six children.

His first wife was Katila Bint Abduluzza. Abu Bakr divorced her during the time of ignorance. Following the divorce, she came to visit her daughter Asma with gifts. Asma refused to accept her gifts and tried to stop her from entering the house. After the incident, Katila spoke to Aisha so that she could speak to the noble Messenger in regards to finding a solution to the matter. Later on, vers-

---

[141] *Sahih Bukhari*, 1/27 (327)

es informed believers that such a relationship was permitted in situations of truce and peace.[142]

After Katila, Abu Bakr married Ummu Ruman Bint Amir, who was the mother of Aisha and Abdurrahman. Ummu Ruman had embraced Islam before her marriage to Abu Bakr. She had made her pledge to the noble Prophet at Mecca. Ummu Ruman passed away in the sixth year of the great migration.

After the death of Ummu Ruman, Abu Bakr married Asma Bint Umays. She was the widow of Ja'far Ibn Abu Talib who was martyred during the battle of Muta. From this marriage, Abu Bakr's youngest son Muhammad was born.

Asma was amongst first women who embraced Islam. She had become a Muslim even before the noble Messenger had entered the house of Ibn Arqam. She was also in the group of people who had migrated to Abyssinia. She had migrated with her husband Ja'far Ibn Abu Talib.

The last woman Abu Bakr married was Habiba Bint Harija. She belonged to the Hazraj clan of the Ansar. Harija was pregnant at the time of his death. She gave birth to a baby girl sometime after and named her Ummu Kulthum.

Abdurrahman was the oldest child. He embraced Islam on the day of Hudaybiya. His efforts during the great migration were extra ordinary. He mingled with the polytheists during the day and then informed the travelers that

---

[142] Mumtehine: 60/8

headed towards civilization about the latest developments in Mecca. He was martyred with an arrow that pierced through his body on the day of Taif. At the time, Abu Bakr was the Caliph.

Abu Bakr's son Muhammad was born on the day of the Farewell Sermon. He lost his father at the tender age of three. Muhammad was raised by Ali. Later on, he was appointed as the Governor of Egypt and was martyred there.

Abu Bakr's oldest daughter Asma, whom the Prophet complimented with the title "Zunnitakayn" during the great migration, married Zubayr Ibn Awwam. Zubayr's son, Abdullah Ibn Zubayr was born from this marriage. Asma was the only woman who was pregnant during the migration. She was the first refugee to give birth in Medina. Therefore, Abdullah Ibn Zubayr was the first unborn child to migrate from Mecca to Medina. Asma died on the seventy-third year of the great migration. She was renowned for her generosity.

Our mother, Aisha, who was married to the noble Messenger of God, passed away on the fifty-seventh year of the great migration.

Before Abu Bakr passed away, he spoke to Aisha about Ummu Kulthum, his unborn child. Abu Bakr advised Aisha about her family members: "These are your brothers, and they are your sisters." Aisha became confused by her father's advice, as she asked: "I understand that they are my brothers and I know that Asma is my sister, but who is my other sister?

Abu Bakr then reminded Aisha of Harija. Just as Abu Bakr had mentioned, Harija gave birth to a baby girl named Ummu Kulthum. Later on, Abu Bakr's youngest child, Ummu Kulthum, married Talha Ibn Ubaydullah.

It is evident that amongst the Companions, the Abu Bakr family stands out with its distinctive qualities. Amongst the Sahaba there is no one that has the characteristics of Abu Bakr. He is the only Companion whose father, mother, and children were all Muslims. Moreover, four generations of the Abu Bakr family had sat down with the Prophet to become Companions. Abu Bakr had achieved this from two different branches of his family tree:

1- Abdullah Ibn Zubayr and his mother Asma, Abu Bakr and his father Abu Kuhafa.

2- Muhammad, the son of Abdurrahman who was Abu Bakr's first son and Abu Bakr and his father Abu Kuhafa.

The final word would be to understand that Abu Bakr was a man who came from the local marketplace and rose to the rank of Caliphate. His accomplishments and the rank he has attained made him a role-model that would never be forgotten by those who came after him.

His life style of constant progress and self-improvement should be taken as a great example by the Muslims of today. He was a model of consistency who never said: I have done enough. He competed to give more and more… On the path of the righteous, he struggled to the end without any hesitation or fear of losing his wealth…

There is only one thing we can say to those who look upon Abu Bakr with envy: "It is not too late! Perhaps you can never be an Abu Bakr, but God willing, you can serve Islam just like Abu Bakr and be remembered for eternity." In order to achieve this, one must first have the intention, followed by an everlasting action…